Artificial Intelligence

Other Publications:
HEALTHY HOME COOKING
YOUR HOME
THE ENCHANTED WORLD
THE KODAK LIBRARY OF CREATIVE PHOTOGRAPHY
GREAT MEALS IN MINUTES
THE CIVIL WAR
PLANET EARTH
COLLECTOR'S LIBRARY OF THE CIVIL WAR
THE EPIC OF FLIGHT
THE GOOD COOK
WORLD WAR II
HOME REPAIR AND IMPROVEMENT
THE OLD WEST

This volume is one of a series that examines
various aspects of computer technology and the
role computers play in modern life.

UNDERSTANDING COMPUTERS

Artificial Intelligence

BY THE EDITORS OF TIME-LIFE BOOKS

TIME-LIFE BOOKS, ALEXANDRIA, VIRGINIA

Contents

7   Rival Theories in
the Quest for AI
ESSAY   Unraveling the Puzzle of Vision

      1

31   Prescriptions for Logical Systems
ESSAY   The Secrets of an Electronic Expert

      2

55   Of Knowledge and Analogy

      3

73   The Learning Challenge
ESSAY   A Robot's Education by Example

      4

99   Seeing and Foreseeing
ESSAY   The Space Frontier

      5

120   Glossary
121   Picture Credits
122   Bibliography
124   Acknowledgments
125   Index

Rival Theories in the Quest for AI

Since the late 1940s, scientists at a growing number of university and corporate research laboratories have been striving toward an audacious goal. Their steps have been slow and frequently uncertain, and they can point to no spectacular gains. But if they succeed, their achievement will almost certainly rank among the most important events in history. Their ultimate aim: to build computers that can perform in such a way that the machines' output will be indistinguishable from that of a human mind.

While the full consequences of such capabilities beggar the imagination, there can be no doubt that the effects on intellectual and technological development would be momentous. The Industrial Revolution, after all, merely amplified the muscles, not the mind. Given their singular capacity to absorb, retain and juggle huge amounts of information, computers might become partners in the enterprise of thought — soaking up the lore of experts, gleaning knowledge from the world's libraries and data banks, discerning deep connections, regularities and contradictions that escape even the most brilliant human thinkers. A machine loaded with enough historical data might, for example, find more workable theories of economics than the obviously imperfect ones that governments now rely upon. Certainly, the appearance of machine intelligence would permit designers to build robots capable of going far beyond the performance of dull, repetitive industrial tasks; it would also make possible the development of computers that can respond to ordinary human speech and anticipate the needs of a user.

As they go about their patient labors, workers in the field of artificial intelligence — or AI, as it is more familiarly known — find themselves grappling with knotty questions that transcend the traditional bounds of computer science. They must seek to understand the nature of learning, of language, of sensory perception. If they are to construct machines that will mimic the human brain, they must grasp the functionings of the brain's billions of interlinked neurons — and many researchers have concluded that understanding the human mind, much less emulating its behavior, is probably the most difficult challenge left in science. Indeed, scientists are actually hard pressed to agree on just what it is that they are striving for, on the meaning of intelligence itself. Like the fabled blind men describing an elephant, just about everyone has a pet definition. To some, intelligence consists of solving hard problems; to others it is learning or forming generalizations or analogies; to still others it is dealing with the world — communicating, perceiving, comprehending what is perceived. Even so, many AI researchers would go along with the so-called Turing test of machine intelligence, proposed in the early 1950s by the British computer genius Alan Turing. A computer would deserve to be described as intelligent, said Turing, if it could deceive a human into believing that it was human.

Given the singular difficulties, the prospects for perfecting a machine that could meet such a challenge seem daunting indeed. But no matter how formidable the hurdles, the quest is sure to continue, for the fascination with creating

Since embarking on the quest to endow computers with intelligence, researchers have pursued two basic approaches, called bottom-up and top-down. Bottom-up theorists seek to build electronic replicas of the brain's neural networks. The top-down school tries to mimic the brain's behavior with complex computer programs.

7

intelligent machines in the human image — devices that seem to think, move, hear, speak or otherwise behave like a human — is strong and deeply rooted. Ancient Egyptians and Romans were awe-struck by religious statues, clearly manipulated by priests, that gestured and spoke prophecies. Medieval lore bristles with tales of automata that could move and talk much as their human masters did. Many a sage of the Middle Ages and even later was rumored to have at hand a homunculus, or small artificial man, that was actually a living, sentient being. One savant, the 16th-century Swiss physician Theophrastus Bombastus von Hohenheim — better known as Paracelsus — left instructions for producing a homunculus by way of a bizarre process that began with burying hermetically sealed human sperm in horse manure. "We shall be like gods," Paracelsus exulted. "We shall duplicate God's greatest miracle — the creation of man."

Interest in such contrivances quickened with the technological progress, particularly in the field of clockwork mechanisms, of the 18th century, though the results were far more toylike than what Paracelsus had imagined. In 1736, the French inventor Jacques de Vaucanson built a man-size mechanical flute player that rendered 12 melodies, fingering the instrument's stops and blowing through the mouthpiece like a human flutist. In the mid-1750s, Friedrich von Knaus, an Austrian artisan in the court of Francis I, devised a series of machines that could hold a pen and write passages of varying length. Another artisan, Pierre Jacquet-Droz of Switzerland, built a couple of astonishingly intricate child-size dolls — a little boy who penned letters and a young woman who played the harpsichord.

Advances in machinery in the 19th century stimulated far more ambitious designs. In the 1830s, for example, the British mathematician Charles Babbage conceived — but never completed — a complex numerical calculator called the Analytical Engine; according to Babbage, the machine would in principle be able to figure out chess moves. Later, in 1914, the director of a technical institute in Spain, Leonardo Torres y Quevedo, actually built an electromechanical device that could play very simple chess end games almost as well as a person.

THE ELECTRONIC APPROACH

Only after World War II, however, did there appear a technology — that of the electronic digital computer — seemingly capable of achieving the elusive goal of simulating intelligent behavior. Regularly referred to in breathless tones as "electronic brains," computers amazed television audiences in 1952 by accurately forecasting election results hours before the final returns were in. That startling feat only confirmed what many scientists had already concluded: Someday, those automatic calculators, so fast, tireless and unerring at arithmetic, might emulate nonnumerical human thought processes, including perceiving and learning, recognizing patterns, comprehending everyday writing and speech, and making judgments in inexact situations in which all the facts are not in hand.

Many of the computer's inventors and pioneer users amused themselves by programming their machines for such nontechnical pursuits as composing music, solving puzzles and playing games; checkers and chess were among the computerized favorites. Programmers with a romantic bent even put their machines to writing love letters.

By the late 1950s, these diversions had evolved more or less informally into the branch of computer science known as artificial intelligence. Confined originally to a few American campuses — notably the Massachusetts Institute of Technology, Carnegie Institute of Technology (now Carnegie-Mellon University) and Stanford — AI research is now under way at many other universities and corporations in the United States and elsewhere. In general, there are two types of AI researchers, each working in a different way toward the development of a thinking machine. One group is mainly interested in pure science: using computers as experimental tools to test theories about how people think. The other group's interest is engineering: finding more applications for computers and making them easier to use. Many in the latter group care little about how people think, contending that this probably has scarcely more relevance to their pursuit than bird flight has to the design of airplanes.

So far, though, both the scientific and the engineering quests have proved to be immeasurably more difficult than early enthusiasts ever imagined. Originally, many artificial-intelligence pioneers thought it would be only a short time — a decade or so — before machines possessed all the greatest human talents and more besides. These canny computers would experience a kind of electronic childhood, educating themselves in the world's libraries. Then, with the speed, orderliness and faultless memory of electronics, they would begin outstripping their human creators. Few people talk like that anymore — or if they do, they do not expect these marvels to be made manifest quite so soon.

AI IN THE MARKETPLACE

Even so, recent years have seen the appearance of many commercial products touted as examples of artificial intelligence. Among them are chess-playing programs that anyone can buy for a personal computer. Some of these off-the-shelf programs can take on chess players of moderate skill, and their sophisticated big brothers, running on larger, more powerful machines, can give human grand masters a good game. Programs called expert systems *(pages 43-53)* now advise people about such things as repairing computers and locomotives, exploring for oil and other minerals, diagnosing diseases and investing money. And AI programs are steadily improving in their ability to deal with the real, sensory world. Some are becoming increasingly fluent in plain written or spoken English and other languages. Many industrial machines now have AI-inspired eyes that can recognize items moving along an assembly line and hands that can pick those items up and assemble them.

Throughout its brief history, AI has served as the cutting edge of computer science. Many now-routine developments, including advanced programming languages, word processing and pattern-recognition programs, were based largely on the work of AI researchers. In short, AI's theories, insights and products are the focus of great interest among people eager to extend the range and power of computers and make these machines more companionable — more like intelligent assistants or perceptive advisers than the literal, stupid electronic slaves they have always been. There can be little doubt that the future course of computation and the impact it will have on society will be set largely by AI research.

In spite of this promising outlook, no AI program so far developed can really be called intelligent in any ordinary sense of the term. For one thing, all are narrowly specialized; the performance of even the most complex expert system more closely resembles that of a trained animal or a clockwork doll than that of a flexible, wide-ranging human. Even many AI researchers themselves now doubt that most such products will prove very useful. And AI has plenty of critics who believe that the field will never overcome these limitations.

One such skeptic is the outspoken Hubert Dreyfus, a professor of philosophy at the University of California at Berkeley. In his view, true intelligence cannot be separated from its psychological base in the human body. "A digital computer is not a human being," he says. "It has no body, no emotions, no needs. It hasn't been socialized by growing up in a community, to make it behave intelligently. I'm not saying computers *can't* be intelligent. But digital computers programmed with facts and rules about our human world can't be intelligent. So AI as we know it won't work."

AN INTELLECTUAL EXPLORER

The drive to build machines that are capable of intelligent behavior owes much to the inspiration of Massachusetts Institute of Technology professor Norbert Wiener, one of the towering figures of American intellectual history. Born in 1894 in Columbia, Missouri, where his father was a professor of modern languages at the state university, Wiener was a child prodigy who could read by the age of three. He entered college at 11 and obtained his Ph.D. from Harvard — with an arcane dissertation on the boundaries between mathematics and philosophy — at 18. Ebullient, rotund, sporting a Vandyke beard, the mature Wiener spoke several languages and was said to be difficult to understand in all of them. He had a broad knowledge of numerous fields besides mathematics, including neurophysiology, medicine, physics and electronics.

Wiener believed that the main opportunities in science lay in exploring so-called boundary regions — areas of study that are not clearly within the purview of one discipline or another, but seem to lie somewhere in between and are thus seldom addressed with the rigor required to reach a solution. "If the difficulty of a physiological problem is mathematical in essence," he explained, "ten physiologists ignorant of mathematics will get precisely as far as one physiologist ignorant of mathematics, and no further." Beginning in 1934, he and a group of other young scientists from the yeasty academic environs of Cambridge, Massachusetts, gathered monthly for dinner at a round table in Vanderbilt Hall, then a dormitory and dining hall at Harvard. Following a sumptuous meal, one of the assembled company would deliver a paper on boundary-region science to good-natured but unsparing criticism. "It was a perfect catharsis for half-baked ideas, insufficient self-criticism, exaggerated self-confidence and pomposity," Wiener would later recall. "Those who could not stand the gaff did not return."

From these sessions and from his own freewheeling studies, Wiener learned about new research on biological nervous systems as well as about the pioneering work on electronic computing machines. His natural inclination was to blend such ideas, a process he began in earnest after the start of World War II, when he worked at M.I.T. on a government-funded project to solve a persistent problem of antiaircraft fire control. By then, airplanes flew so high and fast that unaided human gunners were unlikely to have much luck shooting them down. But Wiener and his associate Julian Bigelow perfected the principle of "automatic feedback control" for new and very effective radar-aimed weapons.

Like the operation of an ordinary domestic thermostat, which causes a furnace to vary its heat output according to household temperature, the feedback principle involves using information from the outside world to change a machine's behavior. Employing sophisticated mathematical techniques, the radar-based antiaircraft predictors that Wiener and Bigelow developed could search out planes and aim the guns by responding to the slightest movement of an aircraft's radar signal. In particular, they were designed to outsmart human pilots: Detecting the start of an evasive turn, they could quickly calculate the plane's subsequent path and direct the gunfire so that the projectiles would intercept the target.

By the war's end, Wiener was so taken by the feedback idea that he made it a cornerstone of theories about intelligence in both humans and machines. In a landmark book published in 1948, he argued that feedback was the means by which all creatures adapt to their environment and accomplish their various goals. Any machine with pretensions of intelligence, he wrote, must also be able to pursue goals and adapt, or learn. Wiener coined the term "cybernetics" for this approach — and for the title of his book — from the Greek word for "steersman."

By that time, other scientists were also pushing the notion that biology had much to teach engineers and designers of computing machines. One of them was the neurophysiologist — and amateur poet — Warren McCulloch, a broad-gauge philosopher-scientist in the Wiener mold. In 1918, as a freshman at Pennsylvania's Haverford College, the young McCulloch had been quizzed by a Quaker professor. "Warren," the professor asked, "what is thee going to be?"

"I don't know," said the forthright McCulloch.

"And what is thee going to do?" the professor persisted.

Still uncertain, McCulloch replied: "I have no idea, but there is one question I would like to answer: What is a number, that a man may know it, and a man that he may know a number?"

"Friend," said the kindly professor with a smile, "thee will be busy as long as thee lives."

In an early fulfillment of this prophecy, McCulloch soon dropped out of Haverford and headed northeast for Yale, where he studied philosophy and psychology and then went to medical school. After doing research in epilepsy and head injuries, he continued with advanced study of the central nervous system. He then moved to the University of Illinois to take over the directorship of the psychiatry department's Laboratory for Basic Research. In 1942, McCulloch attended a scientific conference in New York, where he heard one of Wiener's associates deliver a paper on biological feedback mechanisms. The notion of feedback meshed with McCulloch's own developing ideas about the brain. The following year, in collaboration with his 18-year-old protégé, the brilliant mathematician Walter Pitts, McCulloch proposed a theory about how the brain works — a theory that would help foster the widespread perception that computers and brains function in essentially the same way.

A BINARY VIEW OF NEURONS

Basing their conclusions partly on McCulloch's investigations of neurons — the fundamental, active cells in all animal nervous systems — McCulloch and Pitts advanced the admittedly simplified hypothesis that neurons might be regarded as devices for manipulating binary numbers. Binary numbers, the digits one and zero, are the working medium in a system of mathematical logic. The 19th-century English mathematician George Boole, who devised the ingenious system, had shown that logical propositions could be encoded as one or zero, for true or untrue, and then handled almost as if they were ordinary numbers. During the 1930s, several pioneer computer developers — notably the American Claude Shannon — had perceived that the digits one and zero could correspond to the on and off states of an electrical circuit, making the binary system ideally efficient for electronic computation. McCulloch and Pitts created designs for electronic networks of their simplified neurons and showed how they would be capable of performing practically any imaginable numerical or logical process. They further suggested that such networks might be capable of learning, recognizing patterns and generalizing — clearly basic components of intelligence.

The McCulloch-Pitts theories, plus Wiener's books — *Cybernetics* and, two years later, *The Human Use of Human Beings* — generated great interest in machine intelligence. From the 1940s through the 1960s, a growing number of cybernetics researchers in universities and corporations toiled away in laboratories and workshops, theorizing about the brain's innermost functionings and meticulously soldering together electronic simulations of neurons.

This cybernetic, or neural-modeling, approach to machine intelligence was soon dubbed the "bottom-up" approach: starting with simple analogs of primitive creatures containing a few neurons and working up from there to the human level or beyond. The goal was to create "adaptive networks" or "self-organizing systems" or "learning machines" — terms various researchers used for devices that could observe their environment and employ feedback to modify their behavior, just as behaviorist psychology, a prevalent pyschological school of the time, maintained that living organisms did. The analogy with living organisms was not always useful, however. As Warren McCulloch and his associate Michael Arbib once noted: "If you want a sweetheart in the spring, don't get an amoeba and wait for it to evolve."

Time was not the only factor. A major difficulty encountered by the bottom-up approach in those early days was the costliness of electronic hardware. It was economically prohibitive to model the nervous system of an ant, possessing a mere 20,000 neurons, much less that of a human being, with about 100 billion. Even the most elaborate of the cybernetics experiments had only a few hundred "neurons." Such limitations discouraged many an early researcher.

FATHER OF THE PERCEPTRON

One scientist who remained remarkably undaunted was Frank Rosenblatt, whose work seemed destined to fulfill the highest aspirations of the cyberneticists. Born in New Rochelle, New York, in 1928, Rosenblatt got a bachelor's degree in social psychology from Cornell University in 1950 and earned his doctorate in experimental psychopathology at the same school in 1956. While he was serving as a research psychologist at the Cornell Aeronautical Laboratory, Rosenblatt's special interest in the mechanisms of the human brain led him to seek ways to simulate the brain's operations electronically. In mid-1958, the young scientist staged a computer-simulated demonstration of his so-called perceptron, a prospective electronic device designed to emulate human thinking processes. He said that he expected to have a working model in about a year.

Reporters and others who gathered to observe Rosenblatt's rather elementary exhibition were impressed with what they saw. The Cornell researcher had programmed an IBM 704 computer — one of the most powerful such machines then available — to simulate the perceptron's intricate wiring, which was so complex that the huge computer took about half an hour to perform tasks that the actual perceptron was expected to accomplish in mere thousandths of a second. With an "eye" composed of photoelectric cells, the perceptron would feed signals to banks of electromechanical memory cells that were designed to gauge the relative strength of electrical signals. These were randomly connected to one another in imitation of a then-current theory that the brain absorbs and responds to new information through a system of random connections among neurons. In simulation, the system scanned two patterns of squares and, in a way that Rosenblatt conceded he could explain only in highly technical terms, sorted out the signals and distinguished between patterns.

A GRAND VISION

It was, to be sure, a small beginning. But to Rosenblatt, it seemed clear that the basic principles of human learning had been discovered and that future prospects were all but limitless. "We haven't proved an absolute correspondence with the brain," he conceded, "but perceptron is the best hunch yet." It was only a matter of time, he said, before bigger and better perceptrons would be performing such impressive feats as transcribing oral dictation, translating from one language to another or figuring out solutions to complex nonnumerical problems. In principle, he added, it would even be possible to build electronic brains that would actually be conscious of their own existence and capable of reproducing themselves on an assembly line. Commenting on the perceptron's putative potential, *The New Yorker* remarked: "Our own brain is thoroughly dazzled by the things it's said to do."

Two years later — considerably past his own earlier deadline — Rosenblatt unveiled his working model, the Mark I. Described by one reporter as "little more than a laboratory curiosity," the machine could learn to identify some of the letters of the alphabet displayed on cards before its camera-like lens. This was a long way from problem solving or translation — not to mention self-awareness and reproduction — but Rosenblatt still believed that greater things were sure to come. He must have blanched, though, at the sensationalized accounts of his work that appeared in the popular press. In a story that made the front page of a Chicago newspaper, Rosenblatt was quoted out of context as claiming that his machines would soon be discoursing on the finer points of Shakespeare.

Rosenblatt's work represented a high-water mark in the bottom-up, or neural-modeling, approach to artificial intelligence. In June 1960, he demonstrated the Mark I, a perceptron that consisted, in part, of a bank of 400 photoelectric detector cells, each surveying a portion of whatever image was held up. The detector cells were connected to a bank of 512 vaguely neuron-like association units, each of which combined the electrical signals from several detectors and, in turn, relayed a signal to a bank of response units. The response units correlated all the signals and made a stab at guessing what letter, say, was present.

To make this presumably educated guess, the perceptron employed an elementary form of autonomy, or "self-programming." In recognizing any given letter, some features and combinations of features are obviously more relevant than others. The perceptron could learn to make these discriminations semiautomatically through a kind of trial-and-error process akin to training. When the machine guessed right, its human operator left it alone, but when it guessed wrong, the operator punished it, in effect, by readjusting the machine's electrical connections, weakening the voltage supplied along that pathway. The cumulative effect of repeating this adjustment process a dozen times or more was that the machine eventually learned which features characterized which letter. There was, however, a critical limitation: The machine could not reliably identify letters that were partially obscured, of the wrong size or of a different typeface from those it had been trained to recognize.

A RIVAL APPROACH

Such deficiencies might have been regarded as normal for experimental devices and as incentives to further research. But key figures from another camp of AI researchers grew annoyed by all the attention Rosenblatt and his perceptron were getting. In contrast to the bottom-up camp, this "top-down" school specialized in programming general-purpose digital computers to do things that obviously demand high intelligence in humans — such things as playing chess and proving mathematical and logical theorems.

Among these advocates of the top-down approach were Marvin Minsky and Seymour Papert, both professors at M.I.T. Minsky and Rosenblatt had been classmates at the highly selective — and competitive — Bronx High School of Science in New York City. Inspired by Warren McCulloch's pioneering theories of the brain, Minsky had begun his own career in machine-intelligence research in the bottom-up school, building a learning network of vacuum-tube circuits in 1951. But he had pretty much switched over to the top-down camp by the time the perceptron came along. He and Papert, a South African mathematician who had been introduced to him by McCulloch, devoted an entire book, titled simply *Perceptrons,* to mathematical proofs that perceptrons like Rosenblatt's were inherently incapable of many of the things Rosenblatt claimed they would soon be doing. Far from having the potential to become voice-operated typewriters, roving robots, or machines that could read, listen and understand what they read and heard, perceptrons would never even be smart enough to recognize, for example, an object partly hidden by another object. Seeing a cat's tail protruding from behind a chair, the machine would have no idea what it was looking at.

Minsky and Papert's critique, published in 1969, did not exactly finish off cybernetics. But it crimped the enthusiasm of graduate students and of the government agencies that have traditionally sponsored most machine-intelligence research in the United States. Instead, the money and enthusiasm began flowing into top-down approaches.

To be sure, interest in cybernetics would revive in later years, as the top-down school encountered seemingly insurmountable obstacles of its own. Minsky himself would publicly regret the discouraging impact that his attack had on perceptron-like machines, and his own theories about the requisites for a genuine breakthrough in machine intelligence would call for devices very much like the old perceptron. But for the most part, AI would become synonymous with the top-down approach, the search for more and more complex computer programs to simulate the intricate workings of the human brain.

Unraveling the Puzzle of Vision

Since 1958, when Frank Rosenblatt introduced his so-called perceptrons *(pages 12-14),* AI researchers have been trying to replicate the complex process of vision in a computer. Certainly, any attempt to create autonomous machines that can perform a variety of tasks in a changing environment will require giving the machines the ability not merely to see objects in the external world but to recognize, or make sense of, what they see. Humans do this easily, recognizing familiar objects at a wide range of distances, under different lighting conditions and from almost any angle. That this ability takes scarcely a ripple of conscious thought is precisely the problem from the AI point of view: Human vision cannot be easily studied in a laboratory and is thus extremely difficult to use as a basis for devising computer-vision systems.

A key aspect of machine vision, object recognition, is illustrated on the following pages. Machines capable of recognizing objects could, at the very least, perform such tasks as routine industrial inspection and sorting; they could also be employed to interpret images from satellites that monitor weather or crops, for example.

Any machine-vision system must be able to form, analyze and interpret images. Image formation is straightforward: The computer receives an array of measurements of the amount of light reflected into the system's television-camera eyes from points on the surfaces of objects in the three-dimensional world. Although the computer could simply translate those measurements into an image on a video screen, this would not get the machine any closer to identifying the object. Instead, the system examines the array of numbers, using algorithms that allow it to look for areas where the light-intensity measurements change sharply or in a certain pattern. The goal of this analysis is to extract descriptions that might be used in the identification process. Once the machine has isolated such features of the object as color, shape and texture, it tries to match these features with information stored in memory. Matching is the most crucial aspect of the machine-vision process. Much of the research in this field has been devoted to learning how best to represent necessary information inside the computer and how to design procedures that will let the machine use the information to determine what an object is and what, if anything, to do about it.

Capturing an Image in a Numeric Array

The digitized image of the bear below is made up of more than 245,000 pixels. A small patch from the bear's ear is shown enlarged on the opposite page to illustrate how a machine-vision system records and displays (in gray levels and in color) the gradations in light intensity reflected from different surfaces.

Image formation is the most technically developed stage of machine vision. A television camera records the amount of light reflected into it from the surfaces of objects in a three-dimensional scene. The information is transformed into an electrical signal that varies in proportion to the intensity of the reflected light. A converter then changes the analog electrical signal into digital information for the computer by sampling the signal at regular intervals and translating each sample into a number representing a position on a range of brightness, or intensity, values called a gray scale. The numbers form a two-dimensional grid called a gray-level array;

each value in the array constitutes a pixel, or picture element, of the digitized image.

AI-vision systems commonly use gray scales with values that range from zero to 255; zero represents the darkest and 255 the lightest areas of the image. In color-vision systems, separate measurements are taken for the amounts of red, green and blue wavelengths in the light reflected from the scene. The measurements are translated into three separate arrays of brightness values, each varying from zero to 255. Color systems must therefore process three times as much information per pixel as gray-level systems.

53	50	43	33	27	24	24
50	49	43	34	27	23	23
55	52	48	40	31	25	23
52	52	47	41	33	26	24
52	52	50	46	37	28	24
48	50	51	49	42	31	25
51	52	51	49	46	41	32
51	51	48	45	45	44	34

The numbers in the gray-level array above represent the brightness values of the pixels in the seven-by-eight grid at left, taken from a tiny area of the digitized image opposite. The dramatic shift in numerical values across the middle of the array corresponds to the sharp jump in brightness between the bear's ear and the dark background.

86	80	65	45	32	28	27
83	80	68	49	33	26	25
88	82	76	60	44	30	26
88	88	76	62	47	30	27
86	84	82	75	55	35	28
81	86	86	80	64	43	30
83	87	84	81	75	62	42
88	86	78	73	73	69	49

30	26	23	23
30	26	23	22
34	27	23	22
35	30	26	23
36	32	27	23
40	36	27	23
41	41	41	38	36	36	29
39	36	38	36	35	36	29

28	26	23	23	23
26	25	24	22	22
29	26	23	23	22
28	26	24	23	22
29	28	26	24	23
28	28	26	25	23
29	29	29	28	27	27	25
28	31	29	27	27	29	26

In a color system, three arrays represent the amounts of red, green and blue wavelengths in the light reflected from the bear. The dark background, which reflects virtually no light, shows up as low intensity values on all three arrays.

The Detection of Lines and Boundaries

To identify an object the camera has recorded, the computer in a vision system analyzes the data in the gray-level image, looking first for boundaries — such as between the bear and its background — by scanning for sudden changes in brightness values. The values along the 50-pixel scan line indicated in the bear's left ear are graphed at right.

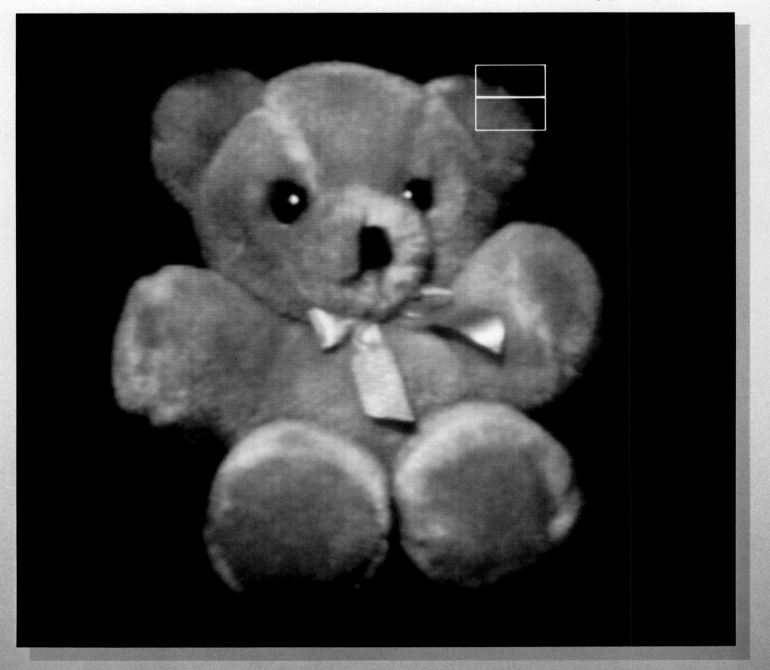

Once the computer has received the stream of numbers representing the varying light intensities reflected from a scene in the three-dimensional world, it begins the task of attempting to decipher what the numbers mean. A common first step is known as edge detection, a procedure that helps the machine find outlines of objects or of parts of objects. The algorithm for edge detection directs the computer to look for the sudden changes in brightness values usually associated with edges such as those that might stem from object boundaries, surface creases or changes in color. In the gray-level image on the opposite page, for instance, major boundaries, such as those between the bear and its background or around the bear's eyes and nose, produce dramatic shifts from dark to light.

The shifts are somewhat masked, however, by a factor called noise — minor variations in intensity caused by surface texture or imperfections such as scratches, and by electronic fluctuations inherent in the digitizing process. Before edge detection can be carried out, the computer must erase or reduce these insignificant values by a process known as smoothing (below). After smoothing, significant changes are plotted to produce an edge picture, or edge map (bottom).

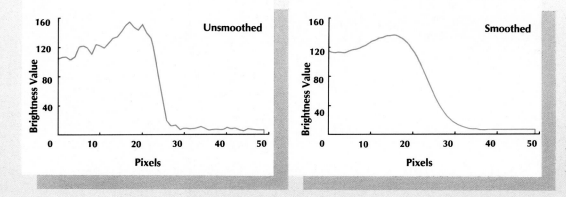

The graph at far left represents a plotting of the intensity values taken from the scan line on the opposite page. These values correspond to minor oscillations in intensity on the surface of the object as well as to significant changes. Smoothing the data produces the graph at near left. In smoothing, the value of each pixel in the array is replaced by a weighted average of itself and its neighbors. The larger the neighborhood of pixels averaged together, the smoother the result and the less noisy the final edge map.

The edge map below shows the amount of noisy detail recorded when intensity changes of more than three units on the gray scale are depicted by dots. The edge map on the right, made after the data was smoothed, yields a clearer outline of the bear.

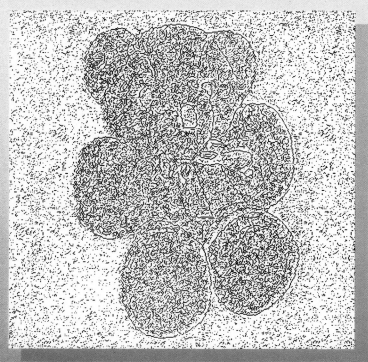

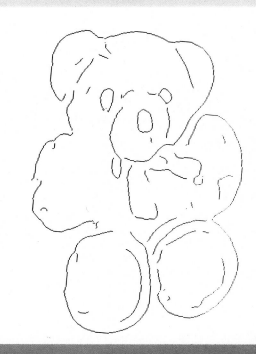

The Problem of Depth Perception

Edge detection is a useful tool in object recognition, but by itself it can yield only a two-dimensional sketch, which will vary with the camera's perspective. In order to perceive depth, machines must have enough information to make a reliable identification of three-dimensional objects.

Humans perceive depth in part through binocular vision: Each eye sends a separate image to the brain, which translates the disparity between corresponding points on the images into a perception of depth. Similar procedures may be applied to machine vision, provided one important problem is solved. A machine can easily be equipped with two cameras to re-

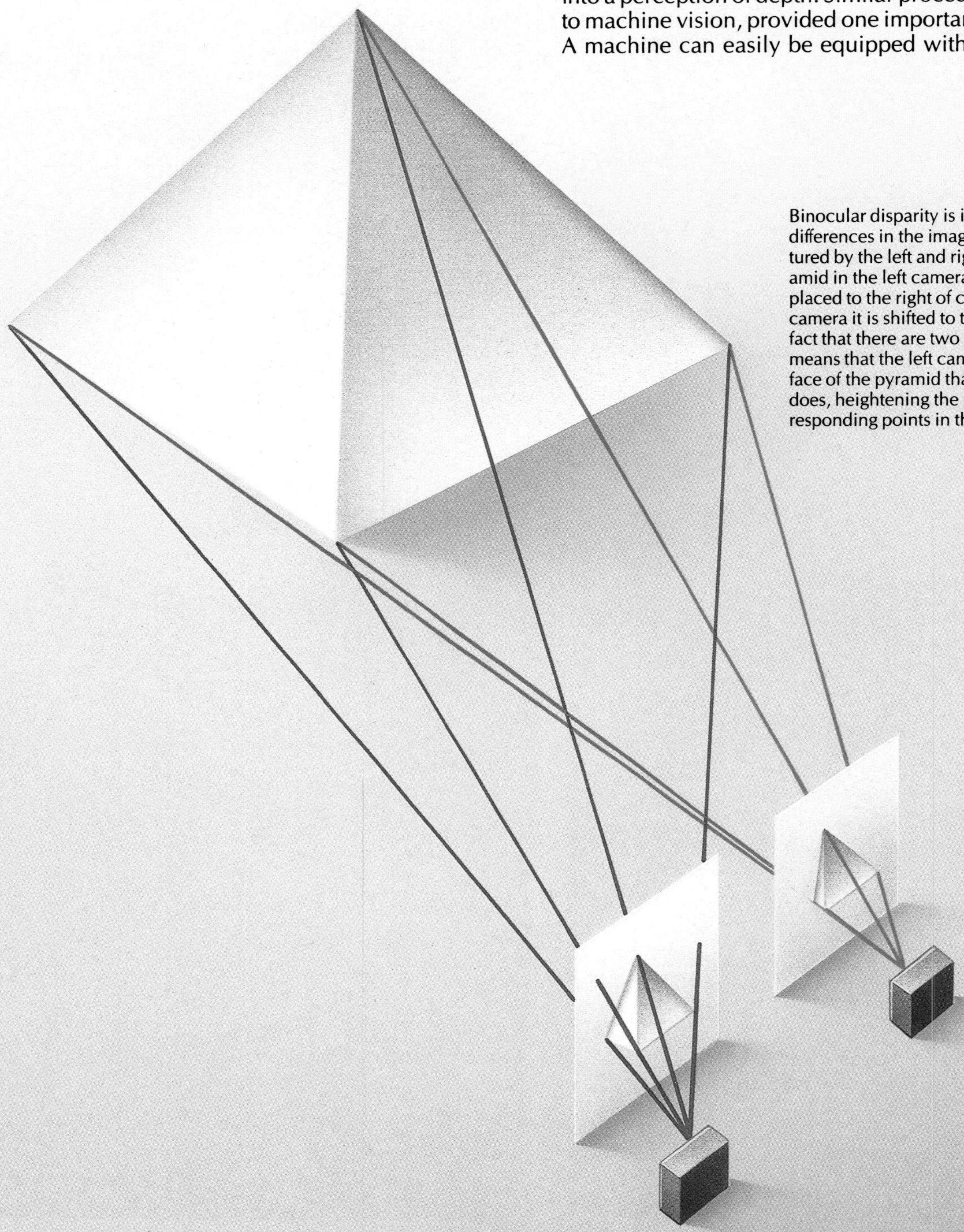

Binocular disparity is illustrated here by the differences in the images of the pyramid captured by the left and right cameras. The pyramid in the left camera's image plane is displaced to the right of center; for the right camera it is shifted to the left. In addition, the fact that there are two different perspectives means that the left camera sees more of the left face of the pyramid than the right camera does, heightening the problem of matching corresponding points in the two images.

cord the view from different perspectives, much as human eyes would. The difficulty comes in identifying corresponding points in the two camera images in order to measure the disparity between them.

This so-called correspondence problem arises because the computer in a system with stereo vision has no clues about the external object aside from two arrays of numbers, representing the brightness values captured by each camera. Not only will a given point on an object appear in different locations in the system's two gray-level arrays, but the values can change with the change in perspective.

One solution to the correspondence problem is to reduce the two gray-level arrays to edge maps through edge detection. The system can then scan the maps for neighborhoods with nearly the same appearance. Once matching neighborhoods have been identified, corresponding points within the neighborhoods can be isolated, and the machine can measure the positions of these points relative to the center of each camera's image plane. From the disparities between the two sets of measurements (box), the system can determine the distance from the cameras to each point on the object and reconstruct a three-dimensional shape, point by point.

Measuring Disparity between Two Images

In this overhead view, the cameras' image planes appear as horizontal lines in front of the lenses; for clarity, the planes are also diagramed at bottom right. As shown here, points A and B, representing the front and right corners of the pyramid, register as separate points (A_R and B_R) on the right camera's image plane. However, the left camera's perspective is such that the two points (A_L and B_L) register as one.

After the computer has identified A_L as corresponding to A_R, it can measure how far and in which direction the points fall relative to the center of their respective image planes. Similar measurements are made for points B_L and B_R. Because the disparity between the measurements for points A_L and A_R is larger than that between the measurements for points B_L and B_R, the computer interprets point A as closer to the camera than point B.

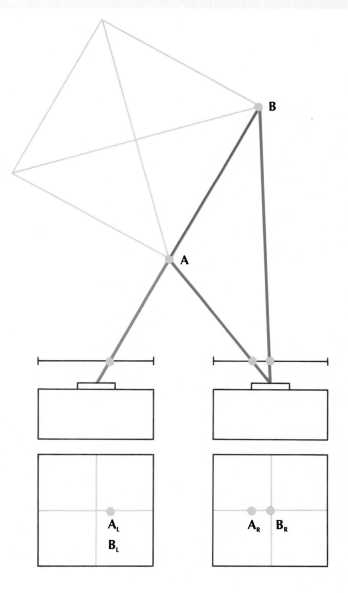

Descriptions of Texture

One of the ways machine-vision systems can pick an object out of the welter of data that represents the external image is by performing texture analysis, a technique that is also applied in object recognition. Because a given texture is represented in the computer's gray-level array as a particular pattern of brightness values, sudden changes in texture often indicate a change in the physical surface, as between grasslands and forest in an aerial photograph, for example. Gradual textural changes can supply clues to the three-dimensional shape of an object.

The surface textures of both corn and pineapple lend themselves well to structural analysis. Both surfaces have characteristic features that are easily distinguished as tokens.

The two general ways of describing the texture of a surface are structural analysis and statistical analysis. In the structural approach, the system looks for salient features, or tokens, and the relationships among them. In an ear of corn, for example, the kernels are tokens that are packed together in rows. In identifying tokens, the system usually applies an edge detector to the gray-level array to look for lines of demarcation.

The statistical approach is employed for textures without easily defined tokens or for images in which such details are not visible, as is the case with some satellite images. The technique focuses on the relationship between a single pixel and its neighbors in the gray-level array, determining the probability that a pixel's intensity value will resemble that of its neighbors. A statistical analysis of the gray-level array of a fur coat, for example, would reveal that a pixel is more likely to resemble its vertical neighbors than its horizontal ones. The texture of the coat, with fine hairs overlapping one another, has a directional quality; as illustrated below, other textural qualities can also be described statistically, including roughness, regularity and contrast.

The hairlike fuzz on a coconut has a directional quality that can be discerned through statistical analysis; the intensity value of each pixel is examined in relation to its vertical and horizontal neighbors.

The surface of an avocado has no features that resolve themselves into tokens; statistical analysis would discern a rough texture, with no directional quality.

The spotted skin of a cantaloupe is full of textural contrast: Changes in brightness across the surface are sudden and distinct. The surface of a squash (below, left), however, has a texture with relatively low contrast; brightness changes are gradual.

A strawberry's pitted surface has a texture that can be described statistically as rough but regular, as opposed to the rough surface texture of the avocado, which is more random in appearance.

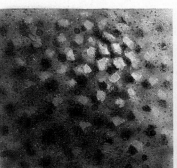
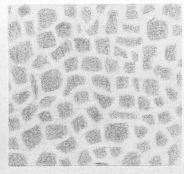
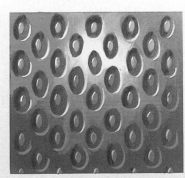

Decoding Color

For machine-vision systems, the main difficulty in identifying objects strictly by color is that perceived color is greatly affected by illumination, a constantly changing element in the real world. Even the apparently simple task of distinguishing an apple from an orange *(below)* becomes complicated if the fruits are in heavy shadow.

Any color has three attributes that are independent of one another: hue, or what is commonly meant by the words "red," "orange," "blue" and so on; intensity, a measure of brightness; and saturation, the purity of the color itself. Illumination changes the intensity and saturation of a perceived color, but hue is relatively independent of changes in lighting.

The camera in a machine-vision system can record only the red, green and blue (RGB) components of a color. Thus, to identify an object's underlying hue, the system must first translate the three color values into measurements of hue, intensity and saturation. The process, which involves several mathematical formulas, is illustrated at right by the three-dimensional model of colors in a machine-vision system. Pure red, green and blue values run along three axes that have as their common origin the black vertex, which is the zero value for all three colors. The so-called intensity axis runs diagonally through the cube from black (no light), through all shades of gray, to white (maximum light).

Strong backlighting renders two oranges and an apple a muddy shade of gray *(above)*. When the effects of illumination are factored out, the fundamental hues of the fruits can be calculated *(below)*.

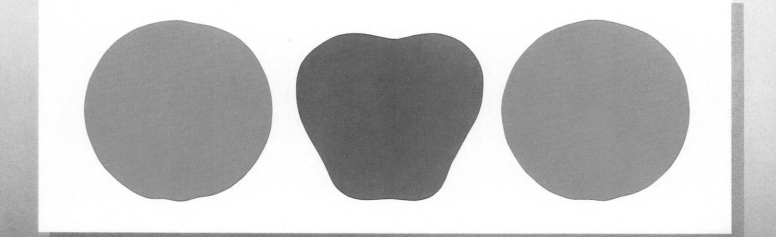

	Red	Green	Blue
Black	0	0	0
Red	255	0	0
Green	0	255	0
Blue	0	0	255
Yellow	255	255	0
Magenta	255	0	255
Cyan	0	255	255
White	255	255	255

Shown at left are the proportions of red, green and blue that make up various colors as recorded by the camera in a computer-vision system. Pure red, for example, registers at the maximum value on the red scale, with no blue or green mixed in; yellow registers as equal parts green and red. Black is, in effect, no color at all, and white registers at the maximum values on all three scales.

To find an object's underlying hue, a machine-vision system must first determine the intensity and saturation of the color represented by the RGB triplet taken from the object's surface. Here, the RGB values come from a spot on one of the backlit oranges at left. Intensity is found by taking the average of the three values and marking that point on the intensity axis. A plane is then drawn through that point, perpendicular to this axis, and the spot represented by the RGB triplet is mapped onto the plane.

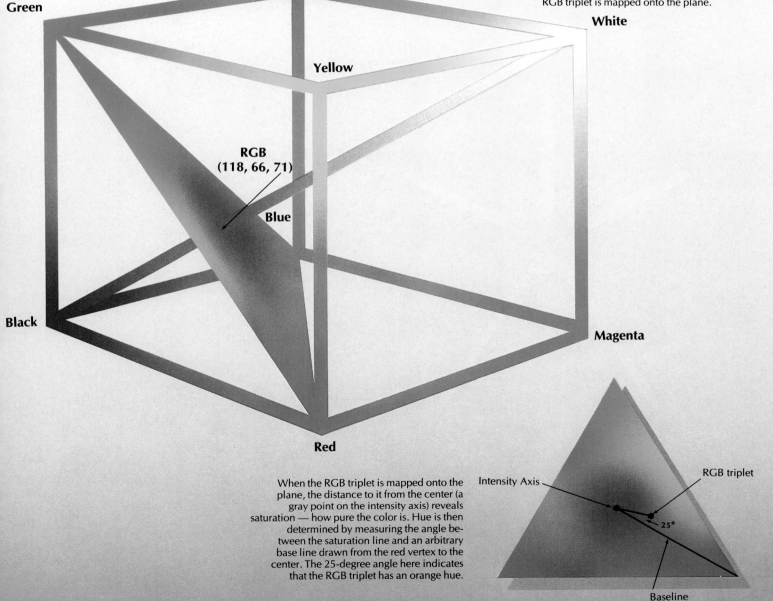

When the RGB triplet is mapped onto the plane, the distance to it from the center (a gray point on the intensity axis) reveals saturation — how pure the color is. Hue is then determined by measuring the angle between the saturation line and an arbitrary base line drawn from the red vertex to the center. The 25-degree angle here indicates that the RGB triplet has an orange hue.

Looking for a Match with a Model

To recognize an object once some of its characteristics have been determined, the machine must match the descriptions of shape, outline, color or texture with models stored in memory. Three ways of doing this are examined here. In template matching, the simplest approach, the machine selects the best match for an object's outline from stored outlines, or templates, of a relatively limited number of known objects. Some systems, such as optical-character readers, which recognize printed characters, store only one template for any given object; other systems, such as industrial robots that can select parts from a conveyor belt, store several. In any case, objects

With template matching, the observed object must fit the computer's stored template of it. In some systems, the image of the object can be normalized — that is, its scale and rotation are manipulated until the image conforms to the template.

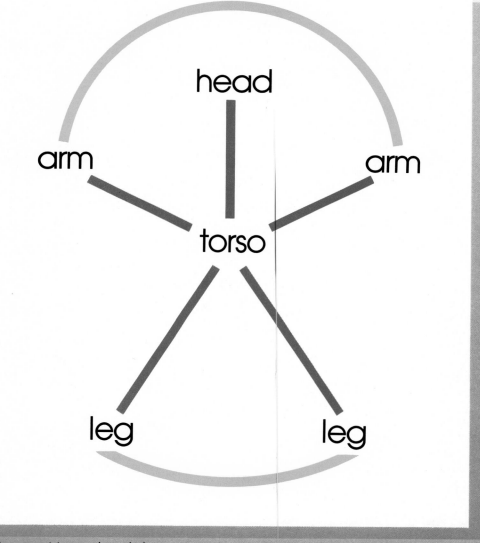

In the connectivity map above, the key components of the human form are linked by blue lines. Orange lines indicate the symmetrical relationship of the arms and legs to the torso.

to be identified must be presented to the camera from a limited range of perspectives; a rotation that renders the object's appearance radically unlike any of the templates would make identification impossible.

Feature extraction allows for more variation from an ideal. The system classifies objects according to certain measurements or features; usually, at least two features are needed. Measurements of color and shape, for instance, are sufficient to distinguish among strawberries, string beans and bananas *(below)*. But to distinguish between strawberries and tomatoes, another feature, such as texture, would be needed.

With the more sophisticated relational approach, the machine recognizes complex objects, which may come in different guises, by looking for the structural relationships between parts of the object rather than focusing on descriptions of the parts themselves. Human beings, for instance, may be tall or short, thin or fat, male or female; they may be seen lying down, standing with their hands on their hips or sitting with their legs crossed. The machine's stored model is called a connectivity map; it represents a person as components linked in various relationships, such as "is connected to," "consists of" or "is a part of."

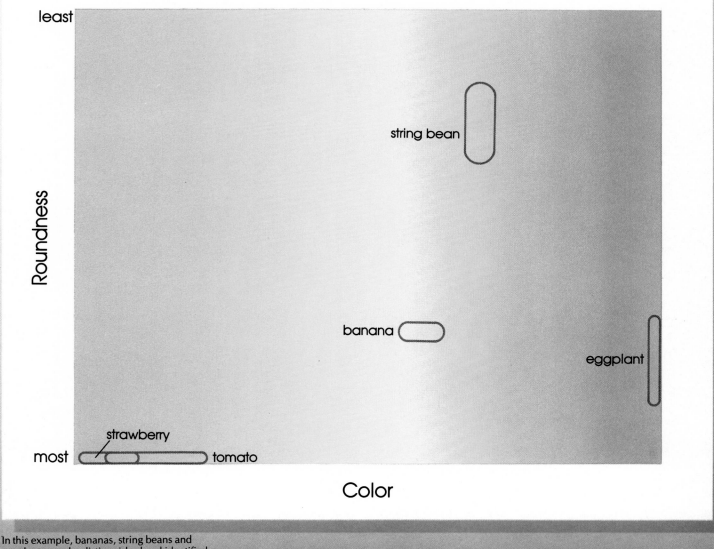

In this example, bananas, string beans and eggplants may be distinguished and identified by their color and degree of roundness. But the ranges for strawberries and tomatoes overlap; to tell them apart, the computer needs another feature, such as texture.

When the Ideal Confronts the Real

Although machine-vision systems are being used in a number of areas, most systems are able to perform only under very constrained circumstances. Optical-character readers, for example, are capable of recognizing characters printed in a specific typeface but cannot make sense of handwriting. Autonomous vehicles can navigate roads — provided the boundary between road and roadside is relatively distinct; such vehicles are likely to wander off into a parking lot if the lot abuts the road. Similarly, machines programmed to recognize objects from a certain perspective will fail if the object

A vision system that stored the image at left as a model for tree would have difficulty recognizing an overhead view *(below)*, a partially occluded view *(near right)* and a transformed view (the tree in winter, *far right)* as the same tree. Moreover, pines and palms *(right, bottom)* are both trees, yet their silhouettes, three-dimensional shapes, colors and textures differ distinctly from those of the prototype.

is presented from a different view. If machine vision is to become truly useful, AI researchers must learn how to represent in the machine concepts that reflect the diversity that occurs in the real world.

Perspective changes are only a small part of the problem, for an object's appearance can be altered in other ways as well. A human being would recognize an orange that has been peeled and sectioned as still an orange; a machine-vision system would know only that the object does not at all resemble an intact fruit. The occlusion of one metal part by another on a conveyor belt might result in the pair's registering as some unknown third object; vision systems still have great difficulty selecting one item from a bin of jumbled parts. Changes in illumination can obscure color and texture and create apparent boundaries, such as shadows, that do not correspond to the real features or three-dimensional shape of the object. Finally, a given class of objects, such as human beings, dogs, automobiles or trees, may have more than one appearance, each of which might fall short of a machine's ideal.

Prescriptions for Logical Systems

In the summer of 1956, a small group of scientists gathered on the campus of Dartmouth College in Hanover, New Hampshire, for a six-week meeting funded in part by a grant from the Rockefeller Foundation. Their purpose was to discuss the problems and prospects of the infant field of artificial intelligence. While the conferees may have disagreed on details, they must all have concurred with the statement of the session's organizers. "The study is to proceed," they had written in their grant proposal, "on the basis of the conjecture that every aspect of learning or any other feature of intelligence can in principle be so precisely described that a machine can be made to simulate it."

Those who attended the conference, which was known as the Dartmouth Summer Research Project on Artificial Intelligence, came from a variety of academic fields and a number of different universities and corporations. But two of them — Allen Newell and Herbert A. Simon — seemed to stand out from the others, not even describing their work as artificial intelligence. Instead, they preferred to call it complex information processing.

By whatever name, the project that Newell and Simon unveiled at Dartmouth was far more advanced than the work of any of their colleagues. And it would lead in time to some of the first applications of AI research to real-life problems. Newell and Simon had little faith in the bottom-up approach of cyberneticists, who insisted that the best hope lay in an analog electronic simulation of the brain's neurons; they maintained that digital computers, properly programmed, held far more promise. For one thing, software could be easily modified, and failures cheaply abandoned. Furthermore, they argued, if AI researchers truly sought to achieve peak human-level intelligence, there would be no point in building simulated nervous systems to do things that humans find trivially easy. Instead, machines should be busied with tasks that place a much greater demand on human intelligence — proving mathematical theorems, solving puzzles or playing board games such as chess.

Simon, a professor of administration at the Carnegie Institute of Technology, had made the first informal disclosure of his groundbreaking research in early January 1956. Strolling into a class where he taught the use of mathematical models in the social sciences, he announced that over the Christmas holidays he and Newell, along with an associate named J. C. Shaw, had invented a thinking machine. Newell and Shaw worked in Santa Monica, California, for the RAND Corporation, the first and most glamorous of the many nonprofit research institutions, known as think tanks, that sprouted after World War II (the organization's name was an acronym for "research and development"). Simon was a part-time consultant at RAND. What Simon and his colleagues had created, in fact, was a computer program, called Logic Theorist, that could prove theorems in the field of pure reasoning known as symbolic logic.

In setting out to develop the program, Simon had not even been particularly concerned with artificial intelligence; rather, his aim was to investigate human

Solving problems in AI involves choosing among sets of options, with each decision opening the door to another array of choices. Programs called expert systems organize fields of knowledge so that a computer can search systematically for a solution without becoming lost in a vast landscape of possibilities.

psychology, only one of his several academic interests. Born in Milwaukee, his father an electrical engineer and his mother a professional pianist, Simon had earned his doctoral degree in political science at the University of Chicago in 1943. His dissertation was based on his study of how certain departments of Milwaukee's city government made decisions. These investigations later led Simon to formulate his theories of "bounded rationality," which held that irrationality plays as large a role as logic in organizational behavior. (Applied in the real worlds of commerce and industry, these theories would win Simon the 1978 Nobel Prize in economics.) In 1949, he went to Carnegie Tech to found the Graduate School of Industrial Administration; later, he would also teach courses in the psychology and the computer-science departments.

If a common thread ran through Simon's diverse activities, it was his fascination with how people make decisions and solve problems. He discovered the computer's usefulness in this regard while visiting RAND in 1952 to help develop training programs for a computer-based air-defense system. What he saw in Santa Monica, he recalled later, "was really an eye opener. They had this marvelous device for simulating maps on old tabulating machines. Here you were, using this thing not to print out statistics, but to print out a picture, which the map was. Suddenly it was obvious that you didn't have to be limited to computing numbers." If the machines had the general ability to recognize and manipulate all the symbols that people use to express knowledge, the computer could become a convenient and objective device for the simulation of human thought.

These notions found a ready reception in RAND employees Newell and Shaw. A native of San Francisco, Newell was the son of a radiology professor at Stanford Medical School. After studying mathematics at Princeton, he came to RAND in 1950. There, he was involved in a study of military supply problems. It led him to some of the same conclusions that Simon had already reached about organizational behavior — that such activities were too complex to be expressed as abstract mathematical models.

Shaw, the son of an Irish-immigrant paint-store owner in Fullerton, California, had left his job as an actuary with a small Los Angeles insurance company to join RAND in 1950. His considerable talent with computer languages soon won him a spot as a senior programmer and would make him a key member of Simon's thinking-machine team.

A LONG-DISTANCE PARTNERSHIP
A few years after meeting in 1952, the trio of Simon, Newell and Shaw began to devise a computer program that would simulate human reasoning. In January 1955, Newell moved to Pittsburgh and enrolled as a graduate student under Simon at Carnegie Tech. With Shaw remaining in Santa Monica to translate his colleagues' ideas into workable computer programs, Newell and Simon engaged in grueling rounds of discussion and planning. Simon later said of these sessions, "The rule was that you could talk nonsense, and vaguely, and you weren't supposed to be called on it unless you intended to be talking accurately and sensibly. You could try out ideas when they were half-baked, or quarter-baked, or not baked at all."

At first, they attempted to build a chess-playing program; then they began to consider geometry. When they found it too difficult to handle the diagrams needed for solving geometry problems, they settled on symbolic logic as a reasonable field to explore. Warming to the task in the fall of 1955, Simon turned to his home bookshelf and a copy of *Principia Mathematica* by Alfred North Whitehead and Bertrand Russell. Published in three volumes between 1910 and 1913, this classic work has served ever since as the bible of symbolic logic, which seeks to manipulate logical theorems in accordance with precise rules.

Simon discussed with Newell the possibility of replicating by machine the mental processes involved in performing such feats. During marathon telephone conversations with Shaw in Santa Monica, Newell oversaw the cobbling of a program that would crank out proofs to theorems such as those posited by Whitehead and Russell. "I thought he was terribly daring," said Simon later, "running up those incredible $200-per-month phone bills." Finally, three days after Christmas, Newell wrote excitedly to Shaw in California that the program actually worked. "Kind of crude," he conceded, "but it works, boy, it works!"

When Newell and Simon attended the Dartmouth conference the following summer, they carried with them the first computer print-outs of their Logic Theorist program, showing that a machine could indeed complete tasks that require intelligence and imagination when performed by humans. In one case, Logic Theorist even discovered a shorter and more ingenious proof than the one that Whitehead and Russell had supplied.

The creators of Logic Theorist had no doubt that genuine thinking machines were imminent. Not long after the Dartmouth conclave, Newell and Simon predicted that within 10 years digital computers would be the world's chess champions, would have discovered at least one important new mathematical theorem and would have written worthwhile music. "It is not my aim to shock or surprise you," Simon wrote in a technical journal, "but the simplest way I can summarize is to say that there are now in the world machines that think, that learn and that create. Moreover, their ability to do these things is going to increase rapidly until — in the visible future — the range of problems that they can handle will be coextensive with the range to which the human mind has been applied."

Indeed, the computer's ability to juggle symbols as readily as numbers made its potential seem all but boundless. And this promise was nowhere more apparent than in the field of symbolic logic, the goal of which is to manipulate the terms in formulas to prove theorems — that is, to deduce facts that are not explicitly stated. Translated into English, one such rule is: "If statement p implies statement q, and statement q implies statement r, then statement p also implies statement r." That rule is the authority for deducing that fire engines will respond to a fire alarm from the pair of assertions: "If you pull a fire alarm, then the alarm will ring," and, "If a fire alarm rings, then fire engines will come."

A PEERLESS SYMBOL MATCHER

In processing such nonnumerical information, computers first translate words and phrases into binary-encoded symbols that can be expressed as on-off pulses of electricity. The machines then rely on their ability to recognize, or match, the strings of symbols. Simon contended that the digital computer's powers at matching such strings and then executing or not executing further operations — depending on how the match turns out — should enable the machine to function in the loftiest realm of human thought, that of deductive logic.

For all its resemblance to a purely mechanical process, however, logic can be a formidably difficult task. Proving a theorem involves selecting the correct rules and postulates to construct a coherent logical chain from premises to conclusion. One possible approach is that of trial and error, a process known in the AI community as exhaustive search. Since computers can search much more rapidly than people can, many early computer scientists tended to place a lot of faith in exhaustive search as a way to solve any kind of problem.

The trouble with trial and error in theorem proving is that even a comparatively small number of rules and statements can yield enormous numbers of possible combinations. In turn, this can set off what AI researchers call a "combinatorial explosion" — a rapidly increasing growth in a problem's complexity as the number of things considered expands *(pages 36-37)*.

Such explosions became evident in the early attempts to write computer programs to play chess. The first such programs consisted mainly of rules for moving chessmen, together with instructions to look ahead and figure out the consequences of all possible moves and countermoves. But it did not take programmers long to see that this was unworkable: The total number of possible moves in a chess game has been calculated to be 10^{120} — a number larger than the number of atoms in the universe. And such a gargantuan job of computation would take even the world's fastest computer many billions of years.

SHORTCUTS THROUGH A UNIVERSE OF POSSIBILITIES

Obviously, human chess masters do not play in this tedious fashion. Instead, they draw upon a wealth of knowledge about chess, gained through study and experience, to narrow the range of choices. One basic rule of thumb, for instance, says that a player should seek to control the center of the board. Expert players concentrate only on lines of attack that promise to help them achieve that end.

Reducing the field of search to practical size is a key to effective planning in many other types of problem solving. This was the primary task of Logic Theorist, although the program's nominal goal had been to show that a computer could operate effectively in the realm of symbolic logic. Logic Theorist's creators touted its ability to tackle complex problems in much the way that a fallible human would — not through exhaustive search but through clever use of rules of thumb and general strategies.

In developing Logic Theorist, Simon and his associates spent considerable time studying how people approach the solutions to knotty questions, such as those found in mathematics or chess. The researchers concluded that people address difficult problems, even those dealing with pure logic, in somewhat illogical fashion. In essence, they use all manner of makeshift tricks and acquired knowledge to muddle through to a solution. Following the lead of Stanford mathematician George Polya, Simon and Newell called such search-limiting rules of thumb "heuristics," a term rooted in the Greek word for "discovery."

The real job of AI research, they proposed, is to discover heuristics and build them into computer programs. In describing Logic Theorist, the authors laid down their goal: "We are not interested in methods that guarantee solutions, but which require vast amounts of computation. Rather, we wish to understand how a mathematician, for example, is able to prove a theorem even though he does not know when he starts how, or if, he is going to succeed."

To defuse potential combinatorial explosions in Logic Theorist, Simon's team built in a heuristic for backward reasoning. That is, the program would begin with the theorem to be proved and then work out what preliminary things would have to be true for the theorem itself to be true. Almost unconsciously, humans frequently use backward reasoning to prevent their activities from becoming aimless. In planning a tour, for instance, we generally have in mind a final destination before we start. We then select a sequence of substeps — modes of transportation, routes, reservations — that will lead to that destination. A similar technique is a central method of science: A researcher first formulates a hypothesis, then carries out experiments to see if the hypothesis is true.

One limitation of Logic Theorist was that it could not tell whether it was on the right track. In real-life situations, people can usually extract hints about their progress, as well as about what to do next, from the state of the problem itself — a form of feedback. In chess, for example, a player might simply abandon an attack that promises to cost too many pieces. Newell, Shaw and Simon concluded that they had to endow their computer programs with some ability to tell whether a search was getting warm. They were so sure they were headed in the right direction that when they sat down to write a successor to Logic Theorist in 1957, they dubbed it General Problem Solver. Usually called GPS, this program employed a method known as means-end analysis, or "hill climbing." The latter term derives from an analogy with climbing a mountain in a dense fog: A useful navigation rule in such a predicament is to choose paths that seem to lead upward over those that seem to lead downward or horizontally.

Given a goal and more data, GPS could sometimes use the hill-climbing approach to make plans. If it was assigned the task of planning trips, for example, GPS would be supplied with such special knowledge as the distances between all relevant points — cities to cities, cities to airports, homes to taxi stands and rental-car agencies to railroad stations. It would also have to know the best modes of transportation for given distances: that planes are preferred for distances greater than, say, 250 miles, trains for distances between 100 and 250 miles, cars between 20 and 100 miles, taxis between one and 20 miles, and walking for less than a mile. GPS would also have to be told much that would be obvious to humans — that a person flying to another city, for instance, cannot take along a car.

STRATEGIES OF PROBLEM SOLVING

With all that information — and much more — stored in its memory, GPS could then devise an overall plan. The program would first break the problem into subproblems and propose subplans for solving them. It might conclude, for example, that the best way to travel from one city to another would be to fly. That would involve planning the best way to get to and from airports, which in turn would involve taxis or cars. A hierarchy of plans reduces the number of possibilities that must be explored, thereby reducing the likelihood of combinatorial explosions that would bog the computer down in endless computations. In planning a trip from city to city, for instance, the machine would consider only flying, trains and driving, not taxis or walking; in plotting moves to a taxi stand, it would exclude flying as a possible mode.

Like the neuron simulations of the cyberneticists, Logic Theorist and General Problem Solver were the result of attempts to isolate universal laws of thought

Coming to Grips with Complexity

Most AI problems require a computer to sift through vast numbers of possibilities to find a solution. A program to plot an efficient itinerary between 50 scattered cities, for instance, must make a series of decisions, with each choice determining what choices come next. Shown here in much-simplified form is one version of a so-called search tree, which branches from a problem's first decision point, through succeeding generations of choices, until a path reaches its logical end.

The method of examining such a tree depends upon the

problem. In exhaustive, or brute-force, search, the tree is explored systematically until a solution is found. This approach, though tedious, is both reliable and practical if a tree is compact enough. But exhaustive search is defeated by the sheer magnitude and complexity of AI problems: The exponential growth of possibilities results in an effect called combinatorial explosion, which can overwhelm even the fastest computers. (In the large diagram shown below, the very act of drawing each branch resulted in the lines' merging at the periphery.)

To make the examination of a tree more manageable, AI workers use heuristics, rules of thumb that guide the search by choosing the most promising branch at any given point. But heuristics are not foolproof. A rule that told a mountain climber always to go up, for example, would cause the climber to reject routes that led down — and the climber could get stuck on a foothill instead of trekking on to the peak. Most problem-solving programs employ both types of search, using heuristics to prune the tree, which is then explored exhaustively.

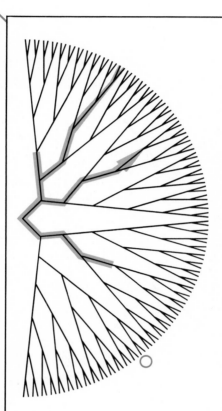

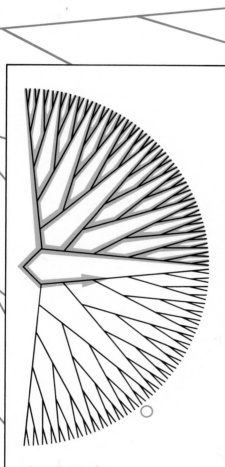

Random Search

Aptly described as the "drunkard's walk," this search method is no method at all. It explores the tree at random, without recording its route. Thus, it often fails to follow a path to its end and sometimes retraces paths it has tried before. A random search might reach the goal *(red circle)* quickly by chance, but it is the least efficient way to go about the job.

Exhaustive Search

By systematically exploring the tree according to a predetermined plan, this approach thoroughly tests every path once, without skipping or repeating any. The plan illustrated above works from left to right, taking the left path at each point unless it already has been tried, and backtracking whenever a path is exhausted, until the goal *(red circle)* is reached.

Heuristic Search

At every decision point, this method applies a heuristic — an evaluation rule that estimates the potential of each option to lead toward the goal — then pursues the most promising option, backtracking if necessary. Here, the heuristic is to measure the distance between a given point and the goal *(blue dot)*, then follow whichever path seems to lead closer.

that would constitute the essence of intelligence. The experimenters hoped that simple logic, simple principles and simple programs, suitable for the limited memories of the computers of the time, would prove capable of tackling many kinds of problems. To endow a system with anything more specific than these rudimentary elements, the researchers felt, would be a form of cheating. It would be a trivial feat, for example, to create a program that told a robot in precise detail how to solve one particular maze: The instructions would merely specify which way the robot is to turn at every junction. But no one would maintain that such a robot — no matter how quickly it performs its designated task — is as intelligent as, say, a rat that painstakingly negotiates the maze by trial and error. Moreover, the rat — unlike the robot — could learn a new solution if the maze were altered; and few people would dispute that the ability to cope with change and to incorporate new information is a fundamental aspect of intelligence.

A MOVE TOWARD SPECIALIZATION

Despite the misgivings of many in the field, the focus of artificial-intelligence research began shifting in the mid-1960s away from simple, general-purpose methods and toward specialized knowledge. In turn, this led to the first programs to be successfully marketed as AI products — though some AI theorists have argued that the programs have little to do with what artificial intelligence should be all about. Known as expert systems, these single-purpose programs are filled with detailed information that enables them to answer questions about certain specialized fields *(pages 43-53)*. Expert systems reflect a realization that general-purpose reasoning techniques have so far failed to do anything very interesting unless humans supply the answers. Edward Feigenbaum, a professor at Stanford and an enthusiastic academic innovator and promoter of expert systems, has said: "We found out that it was better to be knowledgeable than smart."

Feigenbaum, a native of Weehawken, New Jersey, first became interested in artificial intelligence in early 1956. An undergraduate in electrical engineering at Carnegie Tech at the time, he wangled permission to take Herbert Simon's graduate course in mathematical modeling and was at his classroom desk on the January day that Simon announced the development of Logic Theorist. Fired with curiosity, Feigenbaum soon determined to find a career in artificial-intelligence research. After earning his Ph.D. in cognitive psychology, he wound up in 1965 at Stanford's computer-science department. There, as he explained later: "I began to get interested in a set of problems that it seemed to me hadn't been well explored by earlier AI work, namely tasks of empirical induction — given a set of data elements, construct the hypothesis that purports to explain that set of data." A Stanford colleague, Joshua Lederberg, suggested that Feigenbaum might want to try his hand at exploring how scientists analyze organic compounds.

Lederberg — a Nobel laureate in genetics — had his own reasons for encouraging Feigenbaum's interest in organic chemistry. A self-taught computer programmer, Lederberg was working on a more or less conventional program that he hoped would help chemists figure out the molecular structure of unknown organic substances. This was a matter of great moment, for it is the structure, or physical shape, of an organic molecule that primarily determines its chemical properties. Lederberg's first program could predict how different atoms — the building blocks of molecules — might combine on the basis of their various propensities to bind together. But this straightforward approach had the serious flaw of predicting far more molecules than nature itself permits to exist: In the real world, most combinations of atoms are unstable and do not remain intact for very long. Just as Newell, Simon and others had found that they had to use heuristics to constrain chess-playing, theorem-proving and problem-solving programs, Lederberg needed to constrain his program's exuberance with a chemist's acquired rule-of-thumb knowledge about what nature does and does not allow. At that point, he turned to Feigenbaum for help.

Working closely with Lederberg and other Stanford researchers, Feigenbaum began a long and laborious programming task that finally produced an expert system known as DENDRAL. This pioneering program solves intricate chemical problems by playing several types of knowledge and data against one another. One type of data is readings from a mass spectrometer, an instrument that breaks molecules into fragments and measures the weight and electrical charge of each fragment. The program then employs information from chemical theory to calculate all the plausible molecular shapes that could be assembled from such fragments; DENDRAL is also provided with the rule-of-thumb knowledge of human chemists to pare down that list. Finally, the program uses a forward-chaining technique *(pages 48-49)* to predict how each candidate on the list should behave and to compare that prediction with what is actually observed.

DENDRAL was perhaps the first extensive application of another innovation of Newell and Simon's — a system for representing all the knowledge needed by the program as if-then, or situation-action, rules. The if, or situation, side of a rule is made up of a pattern of symbols that the computer seeks a match for. The then, or action, side tells the machine what to assume or what to do when a match is found. For example, an if-then rule of automobile-traffic heuristics might be: "If it is rush hour, then avoid the north-south freeway." Almost any knowledge that can be expressed clearly in words can be presented in if-then form.

THE LOGIC OF A RULE-BASED SYSTEM
A computer program constructed in this fashion is said to be rule-based. In action, it simply plows through the symbols that describe the current situation, looking for patterns that correspond to the if sides of its stored rules. When the program encounters such a pattern, the encounter, in effect, triggers the relevant rule: The program takes some action, such as printing out a prediction or applying a succeeding chain of rules. An expert system for football coaches, for instance, might include the following advice: "If it is fourth down, with many yards to go, then punt." A coach who had to make a decision could type into his game-side computer: "Fourth down and many yards to go" — whereupon the machine would do its if-then calculation and reply: "Punt."

Years of refinement and development made DENDRAL almost as proficient as a human chemist in figuring out chemical structures. Used in chemical laboratories throughout the world, the program has been routinely consulted by researchers who needed to identify unknown substances. Occasionally, researchers even cite DENDRAL as a contributor to technical articles on chemistry.

Spurred by DENDRAL's success, Feigenbaum and others at Stanford examined the feasibility of devising expert systems for additional fields of knowledge — or domains, as they are called by AI workers. One that looked promising was medicine. Edward Shortliffe, a computer enthusiast who had enrolled in the Stanford Medical School in 1970, was so taken by Feigenbaum's work that he persuaded school officials to let him design a course of study that would combine medicine with computer science. Tapping the expertise of several Stanford physicians, Shortliffe set out to create a DENDRAL-inspired expert system that would give advice on the selection of antibiotics for patients. "We tried," he said later, "to capsulize the specific steps that our experts took in the treatment of individual patients into general rules that can stand on their own as overall statements of fact or inferential knowledge to be used when treating *all* patients."

Shortliffe and his collaborators met weekly for hour-and-a-half sessions at which they discussed specific cases. As the physicians explained how they would go about treating certain symptoms, Shortliffe's team would interrupt to ask, "Well, why do you say that?" Then, on the basis of the answers, Shortliffe would devise rules that could be expressed in an if-then format.

With considerable help and encouragement from Feigenbaum and his colleague Bruce Buchanan, another Stanford research scientist, Shortliffe devised an expert system dubbed MYCIN. Armed with some 500 if-then rules for diagnosing meningitis and blood infections and recommending antibiotic therapies, MYCIN was found to perform almost as well as a human physician. One relatively nontechnical sample of MYCIN's if-then process in assessing the results of a bacterial culture: If the infection type is primary-bacteremia, the suspected entry point is the gastrointestinal tract and the site of the culture is one where bacteria are not normally found, then there is evidence that the organism is bacteroides.

ISOLATING THE INFERENCE ENGINE
As they developed MYCIN, Shortliffe, Feigenbaum and Buchanan made a discovery that would greatly expand the applications of expert systems. When they removed the knowledge base from the program — that is, when they took out the specific medical information — what remained was the section containing the logic, the so-called inference engine, or controlling strategy for using the rules. This meant that the knowledge base could be changed or even replaced entirely without affecting the program as a whole. With that finding, it became possible to plug whole new domains of knowledge into the basic program. "We called it EMYCIN, for Empty MYCIN," Feigenbaum recalled later, "but that was the butt of so many jokes that we changed the *E* to stand for Essential MYCIN."

Working with physicians from the Pacific Medical Center, Feigenbaum and his staff soon modified EMYCIN to create an expert system for dealing with lung diseases, and it was not long before this program and others like it were adapted to fields that ranged from computer design to geological exploration and the diagnosis of oil-drilling problems. These led in turn to the marketing of expert-system "shells" — general-purpose inference engines and skeleton knowledge bases into which users can inject their own specialized if-then rules.

For all the potential variety of expert-system applications, more money and effort have probably been poured into medical systems than have gone into all other applications combined. The hope is that the programs will someday be available for use in powerful personal computers, making the world's foremost medical talent available to small hospitals, to remote areas or even to paramedics. One very ambitious project along these lines is the CADUCEUS system, developed at the University of Pittsburgh under Harry Pople, a computer scientist, and Jack Meyers, a professor of internal medicine. Work on CADUCEUS — which was named for the traditional winged-staff-and-serpent symbol of physicians — began in the early 1970s. Its goal is to encompass the essential diagnostic knowledge of some 700 diseases. With Jack Meyers serving as an important source of the system's expertise, it is perhaps unsurprising that CADUCEUS acquired the nickname Jack-in-the-Box.

In tests involving complicated diagnostics cases, CADUCEUS has often scored better on its first guess than have human specialists. Still, it is unlikely that computers will be replacing human diagnosticians anytime soon. Systems such as CADUCEUS are severely limited by the size of their knowledge bases. Confronted with a new symptom or disease, the program will be completely baffled, since it lacks information for dealing with novel situations. A human physician, on the other hand, would be able to draw upon a broad fund of knowledge about illnesses and their various signs, and make connections among them. Pople himself thinks that CADUCEUS and similar programs will be useful primarily in helping physicians organize their thoughts rather than in solving their problems.

PRESERVING HUMAN WISDOM

Some believe that the most valuable role expert systems might play in society would be to help stem the continuous loss of the kind of hard-won individual experience that cannot easily be passed on in classrooms. The difficulty of handing down this knowledge is the main reason for internships and apprenticeships, and for paying seasoned employees more than novices. Unfortunately, the best experts also tend to be those with the fewest productive years left; expert systems offer hopes of immortalizing valued workers' experience in a computer program.

For example, when Aldo Cimino — the Campbell Soup Company's longtime expert in maintaining the complex sterilizers, or "cookers," used for killing bacteria in canned soup — was nearing retirement, management decided to preserve his many years of accumulated know-how in a computer program. The hope was that the program would enable workers to diagnose malfunctions and make repairs quickly, a critical consideration in the soup-making process. As Cimino has explained: "You have only a short period of time to correct the problem. Otherwise you lose the soup."

Cimino spent about seven months with Michael Smith, a so-called knowledge engineer — a computer scientist who tries to reduce complex subjects to the if-then format that can be processed by an expert system. At the start of the project, Smith did not even know what a sterilizer was, but after Cimino spent a few days showing him one of the devices and explaining its basic operation, the two got down to the business of extracting Cimino's knowledge.

"He would ask me 'What goes wrong with these things?' " Cimino recalled later. "And I would tell him. He'd say 'Okay, let's take them one at a time,' so I would tell him step by step what I do when there are temperature problems, or if the cooker doesn't run, or whatever. I told him the solutions I would try for each problem." Finally, Smith put the problems and their solutions into the expert-system shell and came up with a program with more than 150 rules of thumb to aid the operators of Campbell's sterilizers. If soup cans are bent when they come out of the cooker, for example, an operator could look for the reason by typing this problem in at a computer keyboard; the program would display on the console screen a list of possible causes and suggested remedies. After further dialogue with the program, the operator would be able to pinpoint the problem and prepare a print-out to give technicians instructions for repairs.

According to Cimino, this expert system can probably deal successfully with at least 95 percent of the problems likely to arise during normal sterilizer operation. But like its medical counterparts, the program will be stymied when presented with malfunctions that are not covered by its knowledge base. "There is always the oddball problem that will take somebody to analyze," Cimino observes. "In those cases, I used to talk to everybody who was even *near* the equipment. I doubt the computer system can take all of my job."

ADVOCATES AND SKEPTICS
Today, expert-system programming is a full-blown technological craze. Corporations and government agencies are pouring millions of dollars into efforts to develop programs that apply heuristic judgments to problems in areas ranging from computer-circuit design to financial analysis. Clearly, expert systems will have widespread, and perhaps profound, effects on society. Some enthusiasts, in an echo of Herbert Simon's bold pronouncements of the 1950s, maintain that the technology will do as much to spread the effectiveness of society's best experts as did the invention of the printing press.

Others, however, are not quite so sure, holding that rule-based expert systems are too narrow and rigid to be of much use outside a few specialized applications, that they are more akin to the 18th century's inflexible clockwork dolls than they are genuine aids to human judgment. "These programs are exciting, but most of them are not very deep," says Marvin Minsky of M.I.T. "You don't see researchers working on the problem of common-sense reasoning, for instance. There is no program around today that will tell the difference between a dish and a cup."

Despite claims by proponents of expert systems that most human knowledge can be represented in sets of if-then rules, many AI experts are convinced that these representations are too simple for practical use; people do not carry their knowledge around in the form of a list of rules but rather as complex organized structures.

Finally, there remains the problem of discovering and writing all those rules. One of the key findings of AI research is that experts and nonexperts alike find it very difficult to express their knowledge. They know what they know, but they do not know precisely how to say it: A competent automobile driver, asked how far before an intersection to begin applying the brakes under various speed and road conditions, will be hard pressed to provide a ready, articulate answer. Many other kinds of knowledge are equally ineffable. Why, for example, do some individuals seem untrustworthy at first glance, or why are some things simply more interesting than others? The answers to such questions lie buried in the human mind, formed by unconscious skills and knowledge learned through long experience. And in their continuing effort to fulfill the dreams of the 1956 Dartmouth conference on artificial intelligence, numerous scientists are seeking to plumb the learning process and divine how the mind makes its instant, intuitive judgments.

The Secrets of an Electronic Expert

Expert systems — computer programs designed to supply both the knowledge and the reasoning of human experts in a given field — may well be the consultants of the future. They have already been used in such diverse areas as mineral exploration and computer manufacturing. Most often, a system is employed by an expert or an experienced worker as a supplemental source of information and advice. As such systems develop in other areas, they may be used by nonexperts as well.

A typical expert system is composed of two parts, called the knowledge base and the inference engine. The knowledge base is made up of facts — sometimes thousands of them — and rules of thumb known as heuristics. The inference engine manipulates the information in the knowledge base, determining in what order to make associations and inferences. The knowledge base can easily be modified or even replaced without affecting the system's inference process.

To create the store of information at the heart of an expert system, a specialist known as a knowledge engineer works with a human expert to extract every detail of how the expert handles different situations in the particular field. The knowledge engineer then translates these details into a form the computer can readily manipulate and decides how best to link the various mental associations a human expert makes when confronted with a problem. In some instances, the connections may take the form of semantic networks *(pages 62-63)* or frames *(pages 66-67)*. But most expert systems are rule-based: The human expert's knowledge is reformulated as a series of if-then rules. In a very simple medical system, for example, one rule might be "If the patient has a sore throat, a runny nose and is sneezing, then the patient has a cold." Rule-based systems may look for a match between information the user enters ("sore throat") and rules that contain that piece of data, or ask for information to confirm or disprove a hypothesis the user has put forth ("I think the patient has a cold").

On the following pages, a fictional novice detective will turn to an expert-system program to solve a murder. Although the system is greatly simplified for clarity, it nonetheless suggests how a rule-based system might serve as a valuable aid in a domain where perceptiveness is at a premium.

Murder at Mumfrey Manor

When Reginald Garthwaite, Earl of Mumfrey, was found stabbed to death with his own letter opener on the floor of his private library, the finger of suspicion came quickly to point at nightclub owner Hugh Eastwicke, who, it was well known, had recently been accused by Lord Mumfrey of cheating him out of a large sum of money. Just a few days earlier, a heated exchange on the village green, culminating in Lord Mumfrey's refusal to pay and Eastwicke's threatened revenge, had been observed by a number of prominent citizens.

One of the houseguests at Mumfrey Manor when the tragedy occurred was Dr. Richard Hawkins, a celebrated mystery writer whose novel in progress, *Byte Night,* featured a computer programmer who inadvertently learns about a crime. Though he had never before participated in a real murder investigation, Hawkins was certain that he would be able to shed some light on this one.

It happened that as part of the research for his novel, Hawkins had sat in on the collaboration between an elderly private detective and a knowledge engineer to produce a prototype crime-solving expert system. Hawkins paid close attention as the knowledge engineer painstakingly elicited the detective's methods for unraveling murders and questioning suspects. Only after considerable revision and testing did the detective deem his surrogate sleuth ready for use. Hawkins later bought a copy to help him add realistic details to his story.

Almost as soon as Lord Mumfrey's body was discovered, it occurred to the writer that fate had presented him with the ideal opportunity to test the worth of the expert system. While the butler went to call the police, the rest of the staff and the other houseguests gathered nervously in the billiards room, leaving Hawkins to examine the study where the late earl had met his end. Hawkins began by noting the immediate particulars: Lord Mumfrey had last been seen alive at dinner; the body was found an hour and a half later in the library; a glass that had contained port lay on the floor near the victim . . .

An Astute Observer

As Hawkins began his investigation, he thought back to the moment when the body was found. Who first mentioned Hugh Eastwicke as the most likely suspect? And who pointed out the footprints in the snow just outside the french doors, which were slightly ajar? The prints bore the mark of the distinctive left heel that Eastwicke wore to accommodate a wound he had received in the war.

Virtually everyone present concluded that Lord Mumfrey, as was his habit, had retired to the study after dinner to peruse a volume of Proust. Upon hearing a knock at the french doors, he had risen to admit Eastwicke, who lived a quarter mile away, across an open field. The argument between the two had resumed, resulting in Eastwicke's snatching up a letter opener from the desk and thrusting it into the earl's rib cage.

This explanation seemed to satisfy Sergeant Blatters, who arrived with a constable in tow and questioned everyone in the house. But Hawkins was bedeviled by doubts. Retrieving the expert-system program from the glove box of his car, he put the disk in Lord Mumfrey's home computer and set about using it to weigh the likelihood of Eastwicke's guilt.

Hawkins knew that one of the first steps in narrowing the search for a murderer would be to determine from clues at the scene of the crime whether the killer was a stranger or, if not a stranger, someone the victim trusted. Eastwicke and Lord Mumfrey were publicly acknowledged to be enemies; yet, it seemed to Hawkins, the spilled port indicated that the earl had been calmly holding the glass when the killer struck. Would he have been so relaxed in the presence of the likes of Hugh Eastwicke? As Hawkins began to answer the series of questions that flashed on the computer screen, other details of the murder began to come into focus.

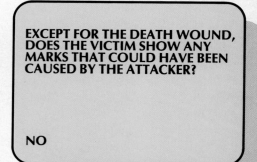

The dialogue between Hawkins and the expert system appears on the screens at right. Given the question Hawkins wanted answered — whether "the victim knew and trusted the killer" — the program called up related questions from its knowledge base. Here, the system asks for specific information about the crime scene and the victim's body that will enable it to construct a chain of reasoning to support its ultimate determination.

HAS THE FURNITURE BEEN DISTURBED?

NO

EXCEPT FOR THE DEATH WOUND, DOES THE VICTIM SHOW ANY MARKS THAT COULD HAVE BEEN CAUSED BY THE ATTACKER?

NO

ARE THERE FOOTPRINTS FROM THE OUTSIDE TO THE BODY?

NO

ARE THE WINDOWS AND OUTER DOORS LOCKED AND FREE OF SIGNS OF TAMPERING?

NO

DID THE CRIME OCCUR IN THE VICTIM'S STUDY, BEDROOM OR DRESSING ROOM?

YES

A Chain of Logic

Sergeant Blatters was impatient, but Hawkins kept tapping at the computer. He was thinking about the hundreds of if-then rules in the system's knowledge base. Rule-based systems use one or a combination of two inference procedures, called forward and backward chaining, to work through the rules. Forward chaining begins with data and reasons from it to a solution. In effect, the user enters information and then asks the system "What conclusions can you draw?" If the user has entered fact A, for example, the system will search for a rule reading "If A, then B," then for one reading "If B, then C," and so on. Backward chaining, the procedure used by Hawkins' system, takes the opposite tack. Given a conclusion — in this case, that "the victim knew and trusted the killer" — the system tries to prove it by following the logic chain backward. If

D is the conclusion, the system will look for any rules that read "If C, then D," then for rules reading "If B, then C." When the system reaches a rule whose if portion is not the conclusion of another rule, it begins asking for specific information.

In Hawkins' case, the system asked about knocked-over furniture and scratches on the body. Hawkins typed "No" to both queries: No furniture had been disturbed, and according to the butler, some scratches on Lord Mumfrey's hand had been caused by a rosebush while the earl was exercising his bloodhound in the gardens. Then the system, chaining down another path, asked if there were footprints around the body. Hawkins answered "No," even though the trail of prints outside seemed to indicate that the murderer had entered and left by the unlocked french doors. But the sharp-eyed Hawkins had noted that the tracks only led up to and away from the doors — no water stains from melted snow or traces of mud from the ground beneath were found near the body or even inside the room.

The writer knew that the system would reveal its line of reasoning if asked to do so. He ran the program again, but now, when the system asked a question, he typed in "Why?" instead of "Yes" or "No" — meaning "Why are you asking this question?" Hawkins could also review the system's conclusion by typing "How?" — meaning "How did you arrive at this conclusion?" The system would then list all the if-then rules it had used. Working with Hawkins' answers to its queries, the system decided that the victim in this case had, in fact, known and trusted his killer.

THE RULES

1) **IF** the victim did not struggle **AND** there is no sign of a break-in **AND** the crime occurred in the victim's private domain, **THEN** the victim knew and trusted the killer.

2) **IF** the furniture is undisturbed **AND,** except for the wound, the victim is free of marks from the attacker, **THEN** the victim did not struggle.

3) **IF** the windows and outer doors are locked and free of signs of tampering **OR** no footprints lead from outside to the victim's body, **THEN** there is no sign of a break-in.

4) **IF** the crime occurred in the victim's study **OR** bedroom **OR** dressing room, **THEN** the crime occurred in the victim's private domain.

This chart illustrates the relationship between the if-then rules the expert system used to determine whether "the victim knew and trusted the killer" *(left)*. If two or more branches of a rule are linked by the word "AND," then all branches must be true for that rule to be true; if they are linked by the word "OR," only one branch must be true for the rule to be true. The red arrows show the beginning of the backward-chaining process.

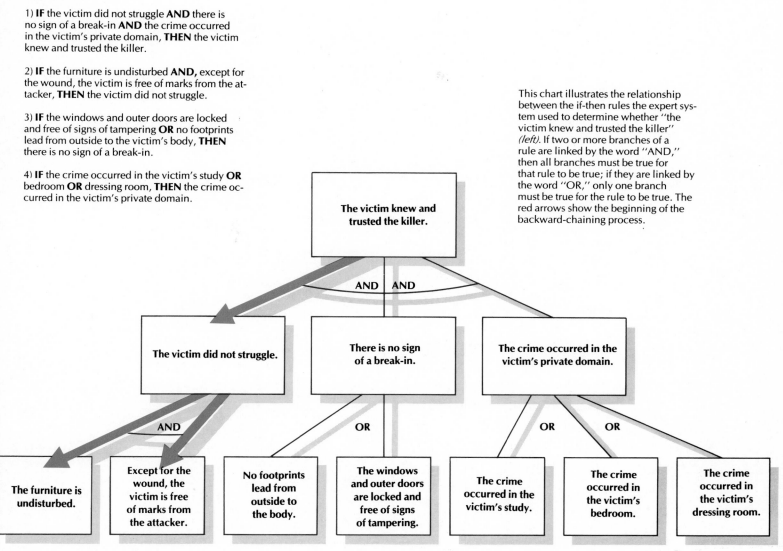

Dealing with Uncertainty

Sergeant Blatters, having long since formed his own opinion about the case, was waiting only for a warrant from the magistrate before ordering the apprehension of Hugh Eastwicke. Concerned that an innocent man was about to be wrongly arrested, Hawkins prepared to make his own case to the sergeant, based on the conclusion reached by the expert system. Like many such systems, the one so carefully constructed by the elderly detective and the knowledge engineer assigned numerical values to the reliability of evidence and inferences so that the user could judge the validity of the system's conclusions.

As Hawkins well knew, a detective in the real world often deals with partial or uncertain information — a smudged fingerprint, say, or questionable testimony — that can affect the validity of the detective's own rules of thumb. Expert systems accommodate such difficulties through the use of so-called certainty factors (CFs).

These factors may be built into the system by the knowl-

The usual procedure for computing the certainty of a given conclusion is shown in the and/or graph below. When two or more branches of an if-then rule are linked by the word "AND," the smallest CF number takes precedence: A chain is only as strong as its weakest link. When branches are linked by the word "OR," the largest certainty factor determines the certainty of the rule. Here, working up from the bottom, the CFs entered by Hawkins are multiplied by the CF of each rule *(circled numbers)* to yield the certainty factors for each succeeding level.

Because the three rules in the second level of the graph are linked by AND, their minimum certainty — .8 — becomes the overall certainty for that level of the graph. This number is then multiplied by .9, the CF assigned by the system to this if-then rule, yielding a final certainty of .72 that "the victim knew and trusted the killer."

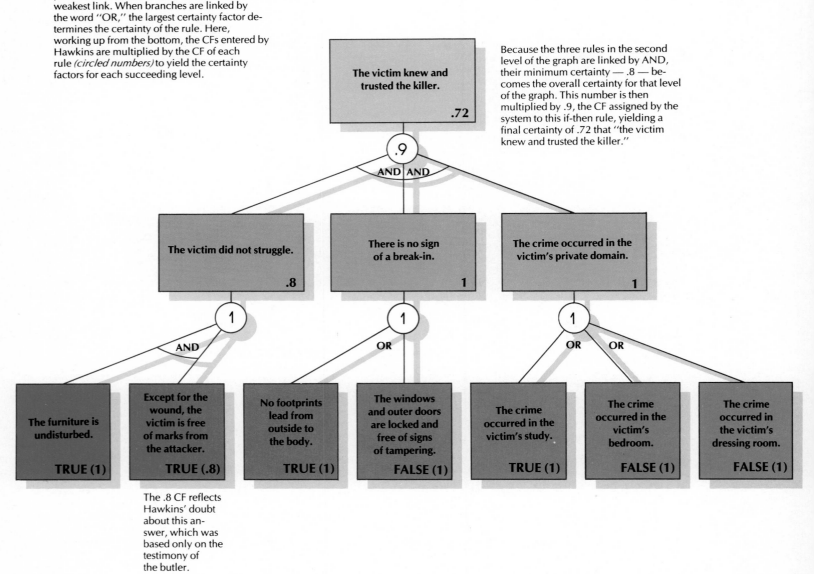

The .8 CF reflects Hawkins' doubt about this answer, which was based only on the testimony of the butler.

edge engineer, based on the expert's hard-won experience. They also may be entered by the user in response to questions posed by the system. A CF of 1 means that the expert or the user is completely certain of a given conclusion, while 0 means "no opinion." A CF between 0 and 1 means that the expert or the user is less than 100 percent sure of a conclusion or an answer. For example, Lord Mumfrey may have gotten the scratches on his hand from a rosebush, as the butler claimed, but when Hawkins answered this question, he decided to allow for the possibility that the butler was lying. So he assigned his "No" a CF of .8.

The expert behind the expert system, for his part, had assigned a certainty factor of .9 to the if-then rule "If the victim did not struggle and there is no sign of a break-in and the crime occurred in the victim's private domain, then the victim knew and trusted the killer." That is, given his own experience, the expert was 90 percent sure that if all three parts of the if statement are true, the conclusion will be accurate.

Of course, the system's conclusion only confirmed Hawkins' first intuition that Eastwicke could not possibly be the murderer: Lord Mumfrey would never have been placidly sipping a glass of port in the presence of the man who had cheated him out of a large portion of his wealth. But if not Eastwicke, who? Hawkins knew he had to give Blatters an alternative suspect. The false trail of footprints led Hawkins to believe that the killer was actually someone who had been in the house, and his thoughts turned to the six people gathered in the next room.

Giuseppe, the cook: His fiery temper was offset only by his extraordinary facility with puff pastry.

Druzilla Towers: Despite her charms, this flame-haired temptress had failed to win a place in Lord Mumfrey's will.

Dworkins, the butler: Lord Mumfrey's faithful servant for more than 30 years was known to play the horses.

Colonel Cleland: In spite of a long friendship, he blamed Lord Mumfrey's poor financial advice for the recent reversal of his fortunes.

Hilda, the upstairs maid: Her mysterious background led some to suspect a blood link to the late earl.

Freddie Garthwaite: The extravagant lifestyle of Lord Mumfrey's ne'er-do-well nephew had left him possessed of debts no honest man could pay.

Unmasking the Killer

Hawkins had to act quickly to prevent Sergeant Blatters from arresting the wrong man. Turning again to the expert system, he quickly fed in what he could about the possible motives and opportunity of the six others who had been in the house at the time of the murder. In the course of the weekend, the writer's trenchant observations had told him a great deal about each of his fellow guests and the household staff. A few quick questions to each of them elicited what he needed to know about their whereabouts before and after dinner.

The system eliminated three whose alibis were watertight. Hawkins now had a strong hunch about the identity of the killer, but he needed hard evidence. Putting his fingers to his lips, he whistled for the late earl's trusty bloodhound, Raoul. He allowed the dog to sniff at the trail of footprints outside the library doors; Hawkins believed the trail to be false, but it might nonetheless reveal the real killer. Scarcely four minutes later, Hawkins' darkest suspicions were confirmed when the bloodhound led him to a pair of Hugh Eastwicke's boots — concealed in the room of young Freddie Garthwaite.

Lord Mumfrey's nephew, who broke down under close questioning, admitted that the day before he had paid a call on Eastwicke, pretending to be his uncle's emissary in the matter of the disputed funds, and had made off with a pair of Eastwicke's distinctive boots. Just before dinner that evening, Freddie went to the open field separating Eastwicke's house from Mumfrey Manor, put on the boots and walked to the french doors to create the false trail. After dinner, he mingled with the other guests, excusing himself just long enough to dispatch his uncle and leave the french doors ajar before rejoining the colonel, Druzilla Towers and Hawkins in the drawing room. By framing Eastwicke for the murder of his uncle, Freddie hoped to hasten his inheritance and rid himself of Eastwicke's claim on it at a single stroke.

As Sergeant Blatters told his constable to take young Freddie away, Hawkins quietly summed up the performance of his electronic consultant. "It is not genius at all," he said, slipping his expert-system disk into the pocket of his dinner jacket, "but rather a simple chain of logic not unlike a trail of footprints. Each new step must follow on the heels of the last until the destination is reached."

Of Knowledge and Analogy

In 1949, the eminent American mathematician Warren Weaver wrote a widely circulated memo describing what he called "the solution of world-wide translation problems." He proposed to simulate on a computer the functions of a language translator. Weaver's idea contained some difficult wrinkles; for example, he suggested the development of a "universal language," which he called Machinese, as an intermediate step in the process of machine translation. Despite that fairly daunting hurdle, Weaver's plan was generally simple and straightforward. Operating on a sentence in one language, the computer would look up each word in an automated bilingual dictionary to choose its equivalent in the second language and then arrange the order of the resulting words according to the appropriate rules of grammar.

The idea struck a responsive chord among linguists, other scientists and engineers. Weaver himself carried impeccable credentials: He was director of natural science for the Rockefeller Foundation. And the computer — though it was usually thought of as a number cruncher in those days — already had shown great promise in a somewhat similar undertaking: deciphering codes. In fact, it was for the purpose of code breaking that Britain's Colossus machine, a large-scale electronic precursor to digital computers, had been invented during World War II. Deciphering another language appeared to be the next logical step. As Weaver put it: "When I look at an article in Russian, I say, This is really written in English, but it has been coded in some strange symbols. I will now proceed to decode."

Officials in the Department of Defense also liked the idea. Eager for an easy way to peruse Russian technical journals to find out what the Soviets were up to in science, the department provided millions of dollars for research in machine translation. Anthony G. Oettinger, who headed a Pentagon-funded project at Harvard during the 1950s, later recalled that Soviet scientists were equally desirous of quick translations of American journals. On both sides of the Iron Curtain, Oettinger noted, "the notion of fully automatic high-quality mechanical translation blossomed like a vigorous weed."

The weed eventually withered. Oettinger himself managed in 1954 to design a computer program capable of word-for-word translation of Russian text into English. But like other machine-translation programs, his mechanical dictionary soon bogged down in the ambiguous multiple meanings and untranslatable idioms characteristic of English and other natural languages (the term "natural" was employed by computer scientists to distinguish written and spoken human languages from the far more formal and precise artificial languages used to communicate with computers).

The computers turned out such gibberish that tales of their incompetence became legendary. One story, probably apocryphal, had it that a researcher instructed his computer to translate the familiar English saying, "The spirit is willing but the flesh is weak." After the machine had processed this into Russian and then back into English, it came out, "The vodka is good but the meat is

Humans acquire knowledge and exchange information through the supple and formidably complex agency of natural language. A prime goal of AI research is to enable computers to participate in dialogue with humans, giving the machines the capacity to understand, for example, that the word "head" can apply to a beaked and feathered crane as well as to a burly bear.

rotten." Other stories were well documented and no less absurd. In one instance, researchers experimenting with translating technical documents back and forth between English and Russian were puzzled by repeated references to a "water-goat." They traced the references back to the English source and found that the machine was merely trying to cope with an engineering term, "hydraulic ram."

By the mid-1960s, most of the funding had stopped and machine-translation projects were sputtering to an end. Translating a language, it was now clear, required more than simply a knowledge of grammatical rules and the meanings of individual words. Before a person — or a computer — could translate from one language into another, he, she or it must first understand that language.

The task of teaching computers to comprehend English and other natural languages thus became one of the first and most frustrating challenges confronting researchers in artificial intelligence. Not least among the problems was defining exactly what it means to "understand." Controversy swirled around a number of questions: Which factor — grammar or meaning — is more important in language understanding? Can such understanding be expressed by some system of formal logic and rules, or does it require huge and complex chunks of the kind of everyday knowledge that humans absorb simply by being alive?

More than 20 years later, answers to these questions remain elusive. Most AI researchers laboring in the field of language comprehension cannot even agree on the aims of their work. Some see their goal as eminently practical: to devise language-understanding products for the marketplace. They want to engineer programs that make it easier to communicate with computers, enabling users to type in their instructions in a natural language instead of in programming languages such as BASIC or Pascal. Others take a more theoretical approach. Because language and thought seem interwoven, inextricably bound up with intelligence, these researchers believe that the effort to build machines that can comprehend natural languages will result in a new understanding of how the human mind works — and eventually in truly intelligent computer programs capable of emulating it.

Language-comprehension programs are thus the focus of much of the esoteric and often acrimonious debate that has racked the AI community for years. The clash of conflicting opinions has been so heated that some presumably scholarly meetings of AI researchers have resembled football games, with partisans shouting and cheering for presentations that buttress their particular point of view.

LAYING THE GROUNDWORK
Well before any of these controversies could arise, however, AI researchers had to overcome a number of serious difficulties in using their machines. Two of the most important elements in improving interaction between computers and humans were easier access to the machine and a more flexible programming language. Both were provided during the late 1950s by John McCar-

thy, then of M.I.T., who actually coined the phrase "artificial intelligence."

One of the four generally acknowledged founders of AI (along with Allen Newell, Herbert Simon and Marvin Minsky), McCarthy remains its most extraordinary figure. Born in 1927, the son of a Marxist labor leader, McCarthy was a Communist during the early 1950s. A decade later, he had evolved into a social radical, complete with long hair and headband. In the 1970s, he climbed mountains, flew planes and occasionally parachuted out of them for sport. By 1980, he was wearing conservative suits and espousing conservative political opinions. He was also rapidly spinning off visionary ideas as fast as he could type them on his home and office computer terminals. A journalist once described McCarthy as "a striking-looking man, silver-haired and patriarchal with a wolfen beard," and went on to note that he possessed "a number of disconcerting social habits — a tendency to walk away from conversations in midsentence, for example."

McCarthy played critical roles in the launching of two of AI's most prominent academic centers — at M.I.T. in 1957 and then at Stanford in 1963. Of his many contributions to the field, his most enduring legacies can be traced to his work at M.I.T. during the late 1950s. There, in 1959, he developed the concept of time sharing, which allows many individuals to work simultaneously at terminals that use the power and memory of one large computer. Among other applications, this meant that AI researchers could write and test their experimental programs on the spot, instead of having to wait for hours or days while their projects were processed in batches of punched cards by a single specialized machine operator.

ADVENT OF A FLEXIBLE LANGUAGE

Soon afterward, a team headed by McCarthy wrote the programming language known as LISP, a playful acronym for List Processing. Unlike FORTRAN, the other principal programming language of the day, LISP was designed to work with nonnumerical symbols, particularly English words and phrases.

Everything in a LISP program is expressed as a list — a set of one or more elements, usually enclosed in parentheses, that may in turn consist of a single item or of other lists. A key feature of the language is that both data and programs are simply lists of symbols enclosed in parentheses, a structure that allows a program to treat another program — or itself — as data. This characteristic makes for the kind of dynamic and flexible programming essential to any attempts to reproduce human thought.

The basic tool for manipulating lists is called a procedure, or function, which specifies the operation to be performed. For example, in FORTRAN, the addition of the variables X and Y would be expressed as $X + Y$. In LISP, the same operation would be written as $(+ X Y)$, where the operator — the addition procedure represented by the plus sign — precedes the operands X and Y. Although this notation is awkward for simple arithmetic, it allows many mathematical concepts to be expressed succinctly and manipulated easily. The same is true for nonnumerical symbols. For instance, with the function (SETQ), a programmer can assign a value to something without specifying ahead of time exactly what it might be: (SETQ RAIN (GET 'YESTERDAY 'RAINFALL)) tells the program to get the RAINFALL value from a list designated YESTERDAY and assign it as the new value for the item RAIN. With LISP, the RAINFALL value might be $\frac{1}{100}$ inch but might also be the word "showers" — two different kinds of information. For additional flexibility, LISP lets researchers write experimental programs without having to set aside large chunks of valuable memory ahead of time to hold information that might end up occupying only a small portion of it — or might overflow it.

Armed with the new language and aided by the instant interaction with computers afforded by time sharing, workers began turning out programs that could carry on a rudimentary dialogue with the machine's operator. The best-known of these conversational partners was created in the mid-1960s by Joseph Weizenbaum, a former General Electric engineer teaching computer science at M.I.T. Weizenbaum christened it ELIZA because, as he wrote later, "like G. B. Shaw's Eliza Doolittle of Pygmalion fame, the program could be taught to 'speak' increasingly well." However, as Weizenbaum went on to note, "it was never quite clear" whether or not ELIZA became any smarter.

Originally intended as a general-purpose system able to converse in English on whatever topic had been programmed into it, ELIZA won fame in the version that came to be known as DOCTOR. In this guise, ELIZA simulated the responses of a psychotherapist interviewing a patient for the first time. Weizenbaum chose to base the program on the nondirective school of psychotherapy founded by Carl Rogers, primarily because therapists of this persuasion tend to say very little. Rogerians typically limit themselves to brief questions and neutral observations aimed at keeping patients talking about their feelings. As a result, ELIZA needed to be programmed with only a minimum of knowledge; the patient's own remarks provided much of the information from which the program derived something for the simulated doctor to say.

The flavor of the resulting therapy session is wonderfully illustrated in this excerpt from a typical dialogue between a researcher playing the patient and ELIZA, whose responses are shown in italics, acting as the doctor:

"Men are all alike."
"In what way?"
"They're always bugging us about something or other."
"Can you think of a specific example?"
"Well, my boyfriend made me come here."
"Your boyfriend made you come here?"
"He says I'm depressed much of the time."
"I am sorry to hear you are depressed."
"It's true. I am unhappy."
"Do you think coming here will help you not to be unhappy?"
"I need some help, that much seems certain."
"What would it mean to you if you got some help?"
"Perhaps I could learn to get along with my mother."
"Tell me more about your family."

ELIZA's pretense of understanding the patient was largely an illusion. The machine was programmed to recognize certain key words and patterns in the

typed input. When the computer found a pattern that matched information built into the program, it responded with simple sentences containing the appropriate canned phrases. For example, the patient's reference to "mother" lead to ELIZA's query about "your family." Another of the program's tricks was to transform the patient's comment into a question, much as a human therapist might do.

If ELIZA failed to recognize a pattern, it was not at a loss for words. The program fell back on its store of neutral comments and questions, such as "I see" or "That's very interesting" or "Why do you think that?" Instructions in the program ensured that the doctor never used the same stock phrase twice in a row.

In short, as Weizenbaum himself admitted, ELIZA could understand "in only the weakest possible sense." One writer has likened this comprehension to that of the family dog when it hears familiar stimulus words such as "dinner" or "walk." Weizenbaum later asserted that true understanding had not been his intention. He wrote that he merely wanted to parody a Rogerian therapist in order to examine the illusion of understanding that often arises in human conversation.

Whatever Weizenbaum's intentions, ELIZA's prepared responses were so seductively plausible that they entranced all kinds of people. In various forms, the program fooled the vice president of a computer-research firm and caused an internationally respected Soviet computer scientist to sit down at a terminal at Stanford and pour out his troubles. Would-be patients besieged Weizenbaum with phone calls asking him to put them on-line with his empathetic computer.

All this amazed ELIZA's creator. "I was startled," Weizenbaum wrote later, "to see how quickly and how very deeply people became emotionally involved with the computer and how unequivocally they anthropomorphized it. Once my secretary, who had watched me work on the program for many months and therefore surely knew it to be merely a computer program, started conversing with it. After only a few interchanges with it, she asked me to leave the room."

What disturbed Weizenbaum even more was that some psychiatrists saw ELIZA as a promising tool to alleviate the shortage of human therapists. One of them, Kenneth Colby of Stanford, a friend of Weizenbaum's who evidently had influenced the decision to program ELIZA as a therapist, was particularly enthusiastic. Colby wrote that with ELIZA as DOCTOR running on a network of time-sharing terminals, "several hundred patients an hour could be handled by a computer system."

Colby's idea of computerized therapy appalled Weizenbaum. This, together with the fact that Colby went on to design his own version of ELIZA without crediting Weizenbaum, brought on disputes that ended their friendship. Indeed, the whole episode seems to have soured Weizenbaum on AI research in general. He remained at M.I.T., but as one of AI's fiercest skeptics.

While ELIZA and similar conversational programs of the 1960s pursued the possibilities of manipulating words according to their meanings, other programs worked largely with the form, or syntax, of language. This approach was influenced by the theories of M.I.T.'s Noam Chomsky, a noted linguist who believes that humans are born with innate mental structures into which they translate the sentences they hear or read. Chomsky's ideas appealed to a number of researchers who favored AI systems based on pure mathematics and logic. His notion that a formal, semimathematical model could be made of language suggested to these scientists that they might be able to adapt some of the hypothetical Chomskyan structures to computer programs. Then, so the thinking went, the language-comprehension machine would not have to understand a word's meaning any more than a computer calculating payrolls understands money or work.

In a typical syntax-based system, computers are equipped with large vocabularies and some knowledge about parts of speech. A built-in syntax analyzer known as a parser then uses hundreds of rules of grammar, not unlike those learned by grade-school children, to break sentences into components such as noun phrases and verb phrases. One rule, for example, indicates that the words "the" and "a" are likely to be followed by a noun phrase. Other rules, based on the positions of verbs, help determine what type of sentence the computer is dealing with—a declarative statement, for instance, or a question.

Some researchers grew dissatisfied with the syntactic approach, however. In their view, it yielded no more valid an understanding of language than did ELIZA's stolid system for matching keywords; like the earlier abortive efforts at machine translation, the syntactic approach tended to founder on ambiguity. A favorite example of critics was the simple sentence, "Time flies like an arrow." A syntax-based system would parse it and come up with no fewer than four different meanings, including the following piece of automated erudition: "A particular variety of flies called 'time flies' (not unlike varieties we know of, such as 'bottle flies' or 'horse flies') are fond of arrows."

WHAT'S IN A WORD
Convinced that a grasp of the formal rules of grammar was not enough, these critics began to reemphasize the importance of semantics. The meanings of individual words, they pointed out, are only a small part of this. Humans readily resolve the ambiguities of language because they bring to it an understanding of the context of a given sentence. Comprehension of context depends in turn upon a detailed knowledge of the subject matter. "You can't talk about what you don't know," one researcher has written. "Getting a machine to understand English doesn't simply involve nouns and verbs. Understanding sentences and stories in any language requires considerable knowledge of the world."

An important step in this direction came in 1968 when Terry Winograd, then a graduate student at M.I.T., began work on a different kind of language-processing program. Winograd christened the program SHRDLU, an apparently mangled string of letters that was actually part of a meaningful printer's symbol: In the days before computerized typesetting, Linotype-machine operators used the non-sense phrase "etaoin shrdlu"—entered quickly by running a finger down the first two rows of keys—to mark a temporary stopping place in their work. With his SHRDLU program, Winograd provided the computer with a body of knowledge about one tiny domain, a microworld consisting of an empty box, a tabletop, fewer than a dozen colored cubes and pyramids, and a simple robot arm to manipulate the toylike blocks by stacking them or putting them in the box. All of this, robot arm included, was simulated in the computer's memory and displayed in three dimensions on the screen.

SHRDLU was a milestone—and probably the most complex computer program written up to that time. Believing that the several aspects of language understanding were inseparable, Winograd successfully integrated in SHRDLU the hitherto discrete functions of syntax, semantics and reasoning ability; all three operated simultaneously in processing English, rather than sequentially, as in previous programs.

As a result, SHRDLU demonstrated a remarkable grasp both of its tiny domain and of English. It responded to typed-in commands such as "Pick up the red block next to the green pyramid" by ordering the robot arm to perform the task. This was impressive enough in those days, but SHRDLU could also indicate that it did not understand something. For instance, if the command was vague, the machine might flash on the computer screen: "I don't understand which pyramid you mean." In addition to performing tasks as requested, SHRDLU answered questions about its little world. It could reply to an abstract question such as "Can the table pick up blocks?" because it had been programmed with the knowledge that only the robot arm could manipulate blocks. When queried, it could even explain what had motivated a particular action. It might answer, for example, that one block had been moved in order to make room for another or that a given action had been performed simply "because you asked me to."

Together with syntax-based and if-then logic systems, SHRDLU prefigured commercially available programs that utilize a form of natural-language processing. Known as front-end programs, they allow a user to retrieve information from a specialized data base by asking questions in everyday English. Thus, in reply to the question, "Who are our Midwestern salesmen?" the machine searches its data bank for categories labeled "salesmen" and "Midwestern," performs the necessary sorting operations and churns out the answer. Such ease of communication comes at a high price: Front-end natural-language programs may sell for tens of thousands of dollars.

Impressive as it was, SHRDLU proved to be impotent outside its own domain and impractical to expand with real-world knowledge. Even within its tiny realm, it failed to understand commands couched in anything but the most precise English. The machine balked at hazy queries such as "How many blocks go on top of each other to make a steeple?" It could not make sense of the phrase "go on top of each other," which contains an obvious paradox if the phrase is taken literally. Humans, of course, tend not to take such a phrase literally. They understand the meaning immediately, thanks to the miscellany of fact and intuition known as common sense. Thus, after SHRDLU, many researchers sought to endow their machines with ever-greater quantities of knowledge — not just highly specialized data but something approaching the common sense people bring to everyday conversation. The trick has been to find ways to organize it all and

Semantic Nets: Linking Nodes of Knowledge

The ability to reason, which people use routinely and with ease, requires vast amounts of information about all kinds of things and their relationships to one another, as well as common-sense knowledge about the world at large. To endow a computer with this ability, all of that data must be organized and stored within the computer's memory in such a way that it can be rapidly manipulated to produce valid inferences or to answer specific questions.

One of the most efficient of these storage techniques is the semantic net — a data structure that consists of nodes, signifying objects or concepts, and links, indicating the relationships among nodes. Nodes and links are easily depicted as diagrams *(below and at right)*. Within the computer, nodes actually correspond to records or memory locations, while links correspond to pointers — address codes that send the program to those memory locations.

The most important type of link is called the Is-A link: Such connections organize the knowledge of a semantic net into a hierarchy that allows lower nodes to inherit the properties of higher nodes. Thus, the CANARY node in the semantic net below inherits all the descriptive attributes of the BIRD and ANIMAL nodes above it. This inheritance mechanism accounts for much of the power of semantic nets. Inheritance also conserves storage space in the computer's memory and makes possible a form of deductive reasoning. Although researchers are still examining the way semantic nets handle exceptions to rules, the principles behind nets form the basis for even more elaborate approaches to knowledge representation, including frames *(pages 66-67)*.

In a strictly hierarchical semantic net, information about a superclass, in this case ANIMALS, is made available to increasingly more specific subclasses through Is-A links. These links allow the lower nodes to inherit the descriptive properties of the related upper nodes. By tracing up the path, an AI program can deduce that a piranha is an animal or answer such questions as "Does a duck have wings?"

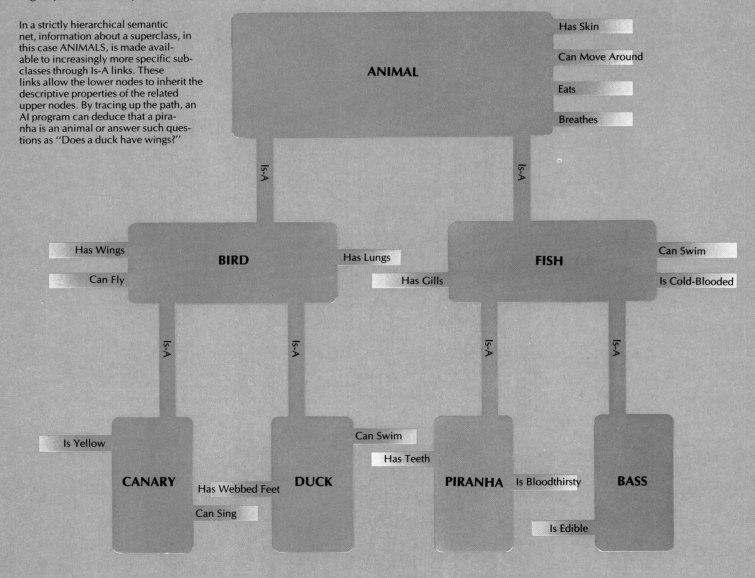

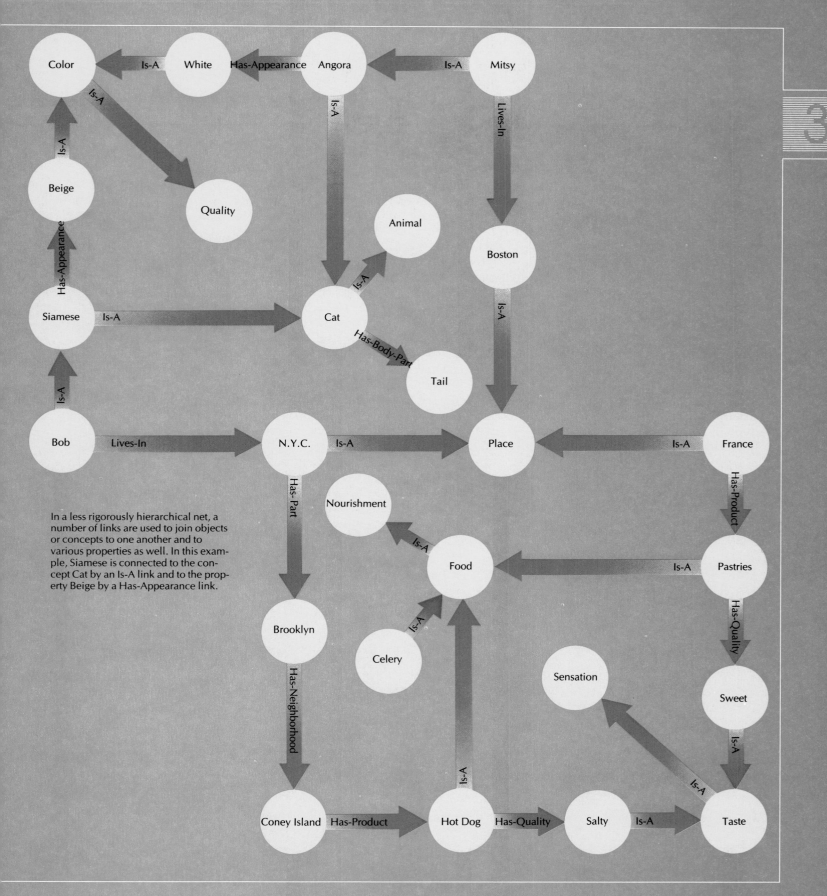

In a less rigorously hierarchical net, a number of links are used to join objects or concepts to one another and to various properties as well. In this example, Siamese is connected to the concept Cat by an Is-A link and to the property Beige by a Has-Appearance link.

represent it in a computer program. Knowledge representation, as the problem is known, came to preoccupy researchers not only in language understanding but in AI generally. How best to achieve it sparked new debates that resembled — and often overlapped — the continuing controversy over syntax and semantics.

Most proponents of a formal, logical approach to language understanding — and to AI research in general — favor the rigorously mathematical if-then method of knowledge representation that has been employed to such good effect in expert systems. Other researchers, who typically favor a semantic approach, contend that if-then rules are too simple to encapsulate all the things that people know and use to help them understand language. These computer scientists work with methods of encoding more complex arrays of knowledge in an effort to emulate the elaborate mental associations that words seem to evoke in the human mind.

As Scott Fahlman, a semantics-oriented researcher at Carnegie-Mellon, has put it: "If I tell you Clyde is an elephant, you suddenly know a lot about Clyde. You know that he probably has two eyes, four legs and is colored gray. You know what would happen to him if you carried him to the top of a building and dropped him off and what would happen if he is held under water for two hours. You know what would happen to you if you tried to hold him under water for two hours. But none of these things is stored in your head under 'Clyde.' They're stored under things like 'elephant' or 'gravity' or 'physical object.' "

This view of how associations are stored in memory — and how a computer program might embody it — was the subject of an influential knowledge-representation scheme proposed by M. Ross Quillian in the late 1960s. Quillian, then a graduate student at Carnegie-Mellon, envisioned human memory as a vast and intricately interconnected web, which he labeled a semantic network *(pages 62-63)*. Such a net, he suggested, consists of nodes that stand for objects, concepts and events, and links between the nodes that specify the nature of the connections. In Fahlman's illustration of Clyde the elephant, for example, the semantic net would embrace a number of nodes and links. The name "Clyde" would be linked to the object "elephant," which in turn would be variously connected to other nodes containing concepts such as "mammal" and properties such as "large" and "gray."

To create a semantic net in a computer, Quillian began a painstaking process of dictionary research. First, he looked up the definitions of common English words; then he looked up the definition of each word in each definition; from this data he compiled dictionary-like lists of cross references in which every word was defined in terms of the others. These lists required more memory than the computers of the day could provide, so Quillian's completed program consisted of fewer than 60 words and their elaborate cross references.

A FRAMEWORK FOR KNOWLEDGE

Though the program failed to live up to Quillian's high hopes — he himself ultimately abandoned AI for social science — the semantic-net concept inspired similar approaches to knowledge representation. In 1974, Marvin Minsky of M.I.T. suggested that the human mind interprets every new situation, and language as well, in the light of mental data structures he called frames *(pages 66-67)*. A frame is a complex package of knowledge — stored in the mind or in a computer program — that describes an object or concept. Each frame contains slots that enumerate attributes and associated values. A frame for a specific dog, for example, might have slots for its breed, sex and owner, along with empty slots to be filled by new pieces of knowledge.

That would be a simple frame. Minsky in fact envisioned far more complex interlocking structures of knowledge in which some of the slots might consist of entire frames, which in turn might be nested within larger frames. Given enough frames, a computer could scan a sentence for symbols that match those in existing slots, thereby activating the parent frame and any related frames. In this way, a system might infer knowledge about a subject not made explicit at the outset: for example, that the dog lives at 40 Chestnut Street and likes bones.

Minsky described his frames proposal in a characteristically breezy memo brimming with speculations — and leaving the details for others to work out. A computerist of unusual breadth, he had been "thinking about thinking," as he puts it, ever since high school. His wide-ranging curiosity was vividly displayed when he was an undergraduate at Harvard. There, he kept no fewer than three different little laboratories of his own, in physics, biology and psychology. And all the while, he was writing an important thesis in mathematics and studying music composition. Even in later years, he would continue to pursue so many interests that colleagues would affectionately refer to him as "the world's best-educated three-year-old."

Minsky's changing ideas about thinking, language comprehension and machine intelligence in general have brought him into collision with his former colleague and cofounder of M.I.T.'s AI lab, John McCarthy. While McCarthy has stood by the notion that even common sense in humans is governed by rigid precepts of mathematical logic, Minsky has come to believe that logic, like

Frames: Packages of Concepts and Data

Semantic nets *(pages 62-63)* are not the only approach to the problem of coding knowledge so that it can be applied by a computer. Another method is to organize information about objects or concepts into complex packages called frames.

The development of frames was influenced by research showing that people mentally file and draw upon their experiences in broad conceptual terms, then fill in the details as needed. The system mimics that activity by providing an over-

BOY FRAME

Is-A	PERSON
Sex	male
Age	under 12 years
Home	a place

ALEX FRAME

Is-A	BOY
Sex	male
Age	8 years
Home	10 Union St.
Favorite Food	banana
Climbs	trees
Body Type	wiry

To conserve space in the computer's memory, frames may be organized hierarchically, with subframes inheriting the properties of related superframes. In the BOY frame above, the first slot acts as an Is-A link to identify the frame's relationship to its parent frame, in this case PERSON. Similarly, the first slot of the ALEX frame indicates that the frame is a subclass of the BOY frame. As such, ALEX inherits all of the slots — sex, age and home — of its two superclasses, BOY and PERSON.

In handling the analogy "Alex is like a monkey," the computer uses one set of heuristics to examine the source frame, MONKEY, for slots whose values might be transferred to the target frame, ALEX. Another set, including such heuristics as "Select slots not already filled in the target frame," allows the machine to choose the best of the proposed analogies. Through this process, the computer can augment what it knows about Alex.

all framework of knowledge consisting of slots to be filled in with specific instances and data. Slots identify properties of an object or concept and contain the particular values associated with each property. In some cases, a slot may hold a so-called default value, to be assumed in the absence of input to the contrary; in other cases, a slot may contain coded instructions that use acquired data to compute a value. Typically, the values stored in slots are pointers to other frames *(below)*.

Like semantic nets, frames may be linked to form a hierarchy that allows descriptive properties to be inherited along the links. AI researchers use frames extensively in attempts to teach computers to understand a natural-language story or to learn by analogy. In the approach to learning-by-analogy illustrated here, the machine transfers slot values from a source frame to a target frame, using heuristics to guide the actual selection of analogous properties.

BANANA FRAME

Is-A	FRUIT
Color	yellow
Taste	sweet
Skin	thick
Source	banana tree

MONKEY FRAME

Is-A	PRIMATE
Sex	one of (male or female)
Age	an integer
Habitat	default = jungle
Favorite Food	default = banana
Climbs	trees
Body Type	default = wiry

Another feature of frame-based knowledge systems is the ability of slots to point to entire frames. Here, the value BANANA in the MONKEY frame directs the program to a memory location storing the computer's knowledge about bananas — a complete frame in itself with slots for color, taste, skin and source. The BANANA frame, in turn, could be linked to related frames, forming a complex, interlocking knowledge structure.

mathematics, is a human invention that plays little part in everyday thinking. "Only the surface of reason is rational," he has said.

Proponents of the logical approach to AI sometimes find Minsky's speculations about the mind mystifying and their implications for machines discouraging. "Minsky's point of view is that intelligence really is built up out of ad hoc schemes held together with chewing gum and baling wire and that somehow they work," a friendly critic has noted. "Now, he may be right, but if he is, I don't think it's a very optimistic point of view because I don't think we'll ever be able to understand or engineer those sorts of things."

If Minsky has become the elder statesman of the antilogic, semantics-oriented wing of language comprehension, Roger Schank is its *enfant terrible*. Schank is the outspoken chairman of the computer-science department at Yale, where he and his band of students turn out ideas and knowledge-representation schemes so distinctive that colleagues sometimes refer to the "Schankian school" of AI research. An intense, black-bearded native of Brooklyn, where he was born in 1946, Schank seldom takes pains to conceal his disdain for work going on outside his "school," which includes outposts — staffed by his former students — at such far-flung places as Columbia and the University of California at Berkeley. He raises hackles with pronouncements that tend to oversimplify complex issues — one such being his division of AI language researchers into two categories, "neats and scruffies."

"Neat people like things formal," he says. "They wear nicely pressed suits and work on surface phenomena like logic and syntax because they can see and understand them. Scruffy people look sloppy and are perfectly happy working on hard, amorphous problems like semantics, just because they're interesting, even if they can't see any possibility of a complete solution."

Schank, a self-described scruffy, approaches his research as a psychologist rather than as a computer scientist. Fascinated less by machines than by the intricacies of the human mind, he studied mathematics at Carnegie-Mellon and earned his Ph.D. in linguistics at the University of Texas. At Texas and then at Stanford, where he taught linguistics and pursued AI research for five years, he balked at the then-prevalent notion that people — or computers — could understand language by analyzing syntax and using formal rules of logic. While still at Stanford, he began developing his theory of "conceptual dependency," which seeks to explain how people comprehend language. According to Schank, people do not merely match words and meanings; instead they translate everything into underlying conceptual structures — a kind of "mentalese" — that make sense of what they hear or read. He points out, for example, that people almost never recall spoken or written words exactly; rather, they remember the gist of what they have heard or read, rephrased in their own words. This conceptual capability, he suggests, enables us to decode with ease such syntactic nightmares as "I hit the boy with the girl with long hair with a hammer with vengeance."

Applying his theory to the computer, Schank invented a language to reduce ordinary English to elementary concepts for representation in the machine. His language distills the thousands of action-denoting verbs found in English to only 11 synthetic words. These hybrid words, which Schank calls semantic primitives, represent action concepts such as movements, speech and propulsion. The primitive "PTRANS," for example, stands for all the ways that an object can be transferred from one location to another, such as by walking or by being carried.

As a result, Schank's programs parse a sentence by breaking it down into semantic elements rather than into nouns and verbs as in syntax-based systems. These elements help the machine decipher relationships in the sentence and resolve linguistic ambiguity. The presence of a PTRANS-type verb, for example, alerts the machine to search the text for clues as to what is moving and where it is going.

SCRIPTING EVERYDAY EVENTS

After coming to Yale in 1974 to launch its Artificial Intelligence Project, Schank incorporated his semantic primitives into a new kind of language-understanding system. First, in collaboration with Robert Abelson, a professor of psychology, he created the knowledge-representation scheme called scripts. A script is similar to a frame that consists of sequences of events, a kind of miniscenario describing what typically takes place when humans engage in such everyday experiences as going to a restaurant or taking a bus. A restaurant script, for example, spells out the usual sequence of entering the restaurant, finding a table, ordering and so on.

The purpose of a script is to help the computer understand simple stories fed into it. The script provides a context, a set of expectations like those that humans bring to a given situation. This enables the machine to fill in information that is missing from individual sentences but implied by the context of the situation. "Ordering a steak is different from ordering a subordinate or ordering your affairs," Schank explains. "But if I tell you it's a restaurant, you don't even think of the other senses of the word 'order.'"

To exploit scripts, Schank and his students in 1974 devised a program called SAM (for Script-Applier Mechanism). The first of several story-understanding systems developed at Yale, SAM uses scripts to summarize or answer questions about simple narratives supplied to the machine. For example, SAM was instructed to process the following little story with the aid of its restaurant script: "John went to a restaurant. He ordered a hamburger. He paid the check and left." When SAM was then asked, "What did John eat?" it replied, "John ate a hamburger." Though this information was not specifically stated in the story, the program could infer the answer from the context.

Another innovation at Yale is the addition of framelike structures to help the machine understand motivation. These various structures — called goals, plans and themes — supplement scripts by explaining human actions in terms of desired ends. Thus, when a program equipped with these structures is told that "John had no money and went to the liquor store with a gun," it can infer that John probably had something in mind other than buying liquor, and it automatically switches over to its knowledge about the motives for robbery.

THE CREATION OF MEMORY WEBS

Though scripts proved useful, they had a number of shortcomings, such as their inflexibility and the narrowness of the situations they could portray. Schank and his students addressed these problems by creating larger data structures called MOPs (for Memory Organization Packets). Unlike scripts, which are isolated chunks of knowledge, MOPs are linked in more complex webs that recognize the similarities between events occurring in different contexts. These memory webs allowed the Yale researchers to construct a program able to answer questions about a complicated tale that required knowledge of several different domains. In one scene of the narrative, set in that favorite locale of Yale programmers, a restaurant, the machine is told: "George was having lunch when the waitress accidentally knocked a glass of Coke on him. George was very annoyed and left, refusing to pay the check." This passage activates parts of several different MOPs, allowing the machine to infer that George walked out without paying because of the atrocious service.

Other programs at Yale have utilized various combinations of data structures to monitor and summarize news stories from wire-service transmissions. One program, armed with the proper script, kept track of terrorism around the world and then made generalizations about the stories it had read. It concluded, for example, that every terrorist attack in Ireland was carried out by the illegal IRA, the Irish Republican Army, and that every hijacking in Lebanon was to protest the disappearance of a Shiite Moslem leader.

A promising program of this type devoted itself exclusively to reading and digesting wire-service reports about one person: Cyrus R. Vance, who served as U.S. secretary of state during the late 1970s. Appropriately, this program was called CYRUS, and someone at Yale even came up with the proper mouthful of jargon to make a true acronym of the name — Computerized Yale Reasoning and Understanding System. CYRUS remembered and analyzed so much information about Vance that it could even provide facts that had never actually appeared in the wire reports. When it was asked whether Vance's wife had ever met the wife of Israeli Prime Minister Menachem Begin, CYRUS hazarded an informed guess. By relying on its knowledge that Vance had once attended a state dinner with Begin and that wives are often present on such occasions, it surmised — correctly — that the wives had indeed met, and it even specified the date.

Critics of Schank's approach to knowledge representation argue that it is messy and unwieldy. They also point out that the Yale programs operate most impressively only in narrow domains of knowledge such as restaurants and the official activities of a single public servant.

THE DEBATE CONTINUES

Many of these critics are engineers committed to designing practical, workaday language-understanding systems based on the simple mathematical logic of if-then rules that has proved successful in expert systems. An articulate spokesman for this point of view is Nils Nilsson, the widely respected head of artificial intelligence at SRI International, a private research organization in Menlo Park, California. Possessed of trim, Scandinavian good looks and a concise and orderly engineer's mind, Nilsson is probably the prototypical neat in Schank's neats-and-scruffies dichotomy.

Nilsson believes that the immense collections of random knowledge required by the Schankian school will prove impossible to engineer. "The whole history of engineering has been to try to simplify and look for principles," he has said. "I think that in building intelligent machines, we ought to at least try to have the same kind of engineering spirit. The issue is whether you believe that there are certain things that are so ineffable that they just can't be described formally."

It may be that everyone is right in such debates, that machines will somehow have to incorporate all of the conflicting approaches — semantic and syntactic, formal logic and Schankian scripts — before they can achieve substantial language understanding. The fact is that despite all the impressive progress, in more than two decades of experimentation, no AI program has come anywhere near the language abilities of the average four-year-old child. Moreover, many critics question whether machines will ever attain understanding in the fullest sense. John R. Searle, a professor of philosophy at Berkeley, insists that computers can achieve only a simulation of understanding, not the real thing. "No one supposes that computer simulations of a five-alarm fire will burn the neighborhood down or that a computer simulation of a rainstorm will leave us all drenched," Searle has written. "Why on earth would anyone suppose that a computer simulation of understanding actually understood anything?" Joseph Weizenbaum, the disillusioned creator of the ELIZA program, makes the point in another way: "It may be possible, following Schank's procedures, to construct a conceptual structure that corresponds to the meaning of the sentence, 'Will you come to dinner with me this evening?' But it is hard to see," Weizenbaum has written, "how Schank-like schemes could possibly understand that same sentence to mean a shy young man's desperate longing for love. Even if a computer could simulate feelings of desperation and of love, is the computer then capable of being desperate and of loving? Can the computer then understand desperation and love?" Weizenbaum answers his own question in the negative and concludes that "even the most powerful Schank-like system" actually understands no better than did his own rudimentary ELIZA more than two decades ago.

The Learning Challenge

In the early days of electronic computing, an all-too-familiar problem for scientists and engineers was that of finding the money to build their machines. Thus it was no mean feat, in mid-1947, for a group of faculty members at the University of Illinois to persuade school officials to finance the design and construction of a computer. But the $110,000 that the university appropriated did not stretch nearly as far as originally hoped. One member of the group, a professor of electrical engineering named Arthur L. Samuel, came up with an intriguing idea. He proposed that they put together a small computer and teach it to play checkers. He reasoned that this novel experiment in machine learning would generate widespread publicity and perhaps attract enough money from government and private sources to keep the main project going.

Samuel chose checkers instead of chess, the game favored by later researchers in what would become known as artificial intelligence, because its rules are much simpler and would require less space in the computer's limited memory. Besides, he recalled many years later, "it happened the next spring there was to be a world checker champion meeting in the little neighboring town of Kankakee. We thought checkers was probably a trivial game. At the end of the tournament we'd challenge the world champion and beat him, you see, and that would get us a lot of attention. We were very naïve."

At the time, Samuel — a genial, dapper man then in his late forties — was carrying a full teaching load and also directing the Electron Devices Laboratory, which had been commissioned to design the components for the new machine. He now embarked on the additional challenge of writing a checkers-playing program. This was new terrain for him. He had worked as a technical researcher at Bell Laboratories before and during World War II and had become an authority on vacuum tubes, the devices that powered the first generation of digital computers. But he knew nothing about programming. Nor, for that matter, did he know much about playing checkers. He did not even like the game.

Not surprisingly, the Kankakee checkers tournament had to make do without the participation of Samuel's checkers-playing computer. But the failed project taught Samuel enough about computers and programming to catapult him at midlife into a new career and into an obsession with what has since become a key focus of AI research: teaching machines to learn from experience.

In 1949, seeking a chance to work full-time on computers, Samuel joined the staff of the IBM research lab at Poughkeepsie, New York. There, he helped design IBM's first line of commercial computers while pursuing development of the checkers-playing program in his spare time. In fact, the growing length and complexity of his program made it ideal for testing the new 701, IBM's first mass-produced, stored-program, general-purpose computer, which was introduced in 1952. Samuel would play checkers on this computer at night, debugging his pet program while trying out the new machine. Sometimes, three machines would be operating at once — being tested "to go into the world," as one computer

The ability to learn through experience is a key attribute of human intelligence — and the most elusive target of AI research. Computer scientists have developed programs that can learn to identify simple shapes, but a challenge like the one illustrated here — recognizing that spheres, cones and cylinders may all cast circular shadows — is far beyond the powers of any present-day computer.

historian put it, "and do accounting, inventory and other sober tasks by playing the game old men play with their grandchildren."

Samuel's overlapping roles as computer designer and part-time programmer eventually led to suggestions — only half in jest — that the logic of IBM's early machines was actually designed to make it easier to represent a checkerboard. Such notions were frowned upon by the company, of course. Under Thomas Watson Sr., its shrewd and image-conscious chairman, IBM tolerated Samuel's extracurricular work but did little to encourage or publicize it. "It smacked too much of machine thinking," Samuel remembered, "and they wanted to dispel any worry people had with machines taking over the world and all that sort of thing." IBM's motto "Think" applied only to employees.

Nonetheless, word about an ingenious program that taught a computer to play checkers got around, reaching even to Europe. When Samuel served there for a while during the 1950s as a roving lecturer on computers in general and on IBM's 701 in particular, the checkers program was often his entree into European computer laboratories.

Samuel never complained about being a prophet without honor in his own company. Back in the United States, he found stimulation by attending meetings on artificial intelligence, such as the famous summer conference at Dartmouth in 1956. But he objected strongly to what he labeled "the bane of AI's existence" — the tendency of researchers to get carried away with exaggerated optimism about the promise of their work. "I was always very cautious," he noted later, "trying not to claim too much."

THE RUDIMENTS OF LEARNING
In keeping with this philosophy, Samuel worked steadily and quietly to perfect his program. At first the machine's ability depended only on what Samuel called rote learning. He programmed in the rules of the game and taught the computer to look ahead several moves and evaluate the potential consequences of a given position by attaching numerical values to various options.

These evaluations were based on heuristics specific to the game, nuggets of checkers wisdom familiar to a player even of Samuel's limited knowledge. For example, a player who is ahead in the game often deliberately sacrifices pieces by moving them into positions that will result in even trades and thus deplete the opponent's supply of checkers. Samuel fed these heuristics into the program, much as a human checkers player might lecture a neophyte, who then retains the strategies simply by memorizing them.

Though different in other respects, Samuel's program presaged today's expert systems, which benefit from the knowledge of specialists in a given field. Unfortunately, Samuel was no expert, and the checkers literature and gifted players he consulted were of little help in spelling out better heuristics. As a result, the program initially could play the game no better than its creator.

Samuel remedied this shortcoming by equipping the program with a better kind of expertise, which he called learning by generalization. He built into the program provisions for remembering and acting upon its experience. In calculating the value of various options, the program took into account the success or failure of similar moves in the past. Thus, the machine was guided not only by built-in heuristics but also by the wisdom born of experience.

Like a human player, it was capable of learning from its own mistakes.

Thereafter, the program started improving some aspects of its play with almost every contest. Soon it was defeating Samuel so readily that he vowed not to play it again until his own game was much better. By the summer of 1962 — 15 years after Samuel gave birth to the idea — the program was playing on the master's level and was ready to take on its first human champion. Samuel challenged Robert W. Nealey, a former Connecticut state champion who had gone undefeated for eight years, and the machine won handily. "In the matter of the end game," Nealey said afterward, "I have not had such competition from any human being since 1954, when I lost my last game."

THE GOAL OF SELF-IMPROVEMENT

Samuel's program remains a milestone in AI research less for its skill at checkers (in 1977, it met its match in a rival program developed at Duke University) than for its remarkable — albeit rudimentary — ability to modify its behavior according to what it experienced. Developing this ability — the very essence of learning — has since become the goal of many researchers, who are convinced that any artificial intelligence worthy of the name must be capable of self-improvement.

Although the goal itself seems clear enough, the techniques marshaled in pursuit of it are all subject to controversy. One issue is simply that of the vast amount of time involved in giving machines enough of a knowledge base even to begin functioning. Another, closely related issue is whether machine learning is really achieved by a program that requires a human to supply its data base and to further equip it with rules that operate on that data. Expert systems, for example, are highly touted in many circles for their practical applications. But even the most sophisticated of them are merely capable of the machine equivalent of learning by rote: Whatever information and heuristics an expert system employs must be explicitly provided by programmers working with knowledge engineers in a procedure so time-consuming and expensive that it constitutes a critical bottleneck. As Roger Schank, head of AI research at Yale University, has observed: "Each piece of knowledge that you put into a computer requires tremendous coding of new information. We simply can't hand-code all these things. Humans don't learn that way."

Such frustrations gave rise to another approach, called learning by example (or, sometimes, learning by induction). A young child learns the concept of tree, for instance, by observing examples pointed out as trees, extracting the essential features that distinguish this class of plants and generalizing from these specifics to arrive at a concept. AI researchers investigating learning by example hope to sidestep the tedious process of programming human expertise into machines. Finding this shortcut would not only speed up the creation of expert systems but also instill in them some of the marvelous capacity of the human mind to adapt behavior to changing circumstances.

Patrick H. Winston, who became director of the AI laboratory at M.I.T. in 1973, tackled the problem of programming a machine to learn by example while still an M.I.T. graduate student in the late 1960s. Winston devised a program called Arches and taught it, through a few carefully selected examples, to recognize simple architectural concepts.

First, Winston supplied the computer with various configurations of toy blocks; drawings of toy-block assemblies were converted into structural descriptions of particular configurations. Then came the learning part: To help the machine identify spatial relationships among the blocks, Winston provided the program with heuristics that enabled it to identify relationships such as "left of," "touches" and "supports." To begin the teaching phase, Winston supplied the machine with descriptions of three blocks that formed an arch and told it, in effect, "That is an arch." Then he gave it so-called near misses that differed in one attribute — a drawing in which the third block is unsupported by the other two, for instance — telling the machine, "That is not an arch."

The program emulated a process that is generally believed to go on in the human mind. It isolated the relevant features present in the positive examples and noted similarities to and differences from the negative examples. After a few trials, the program taught itself a simple but essential concept: An arch consists of a central block on top of two supporting blocks that do not touch each other.

Winston's success with Arches encouraged other researchers in the field, who took his work a step further. Whereas Arches was limited to the world of toy blocks, a program developed in 1976 by Ryszard Michalski and his colleagues at the University of Illinois dealt with the formation of concepts of practical significance. Their program, AQ11, was first supplied with descriptions of 290 diseased soybean plants, including symptoms such as the color and condition of the leaves and stem, along with an expert's diagnosis for each plant. By processing this data, AQ11 taught itself if-then rules for identifying plant disorders from given symptoms, thus becoming a kind of self-programmed expert system.

In one notable experiment, Michalski pitted AQ11's self-developed heuristics against those devised by human experts in plant pathology. The goal of this battle of wits was to correctly diagnose the 15 most common soybean-plant diseases. The researchers consulted leading plant pathologists and translated this human diagnostic knowledge into if-then rules, much as they would in programming an ordinary expert system. Then they typed into the computer the symptoms observed in 340 ailing soybean plants that had been collected for the experiment.

The machine was then instructed to diagnose the diseases in two separate runs. In one run, it used heuristics that had been mined from the brains of the human experts; in the other, it used the rules that AQ11 had formulated on its own after being exposed to examples of soybean diseases. AQ11 won, zeroing in on the correct diagnosis 97.6 percent of the time with its own rules, compared with a 71.8 percent success rate when the machine relied on the heuristics derived from human experts. Later versions of AQ11 were applied in such areas as medicine, physics and chess.

TESTING HYPOTHESES WITH EXPERIMENTS

The self-programming techniques of AQ11 and its various configurations represented a major advance in machine learning. Elsewhere, work began on learning programs that not only perceived patterns in observed data and inferred hypotheses from them, but put these hypotheses to the test of experiment. This self-guided discovery lies at the heart of the scientific method. As AI researchers like to point out, one of their favorite terms, "heuristic," is linguistically related to "eureka" — literally "I found" — which Archimedes supposedly shouted when he leaped from his bath to run naked through the streets of ancient Syracuse after discovering the principle of specific gravity.

Since the late 1970s, the process of learning by discovery has been the subject of a series of programs by Herbert Simon, Patrick Langley and others of their colleagues at Carnegie-Mellon. The programs are collectively known as BACON in honor of the English philosopher of science Sir Francis Bacon, an early advocate of empirical research and inductive reasoning. The historical name is especially appropriate, since the programs number among their accomplishments the rediscovery of many of the most profound laws in science, including Archimedes' law of displacement, which was included in his formulation of specific gravity.

IN SEARCH OF RELATIONSHIPS

BACON's ability hinges primarily upon a small number of heuristics designed to find significant mathematical relationships among the sets of data fed into the machine. Once the program has detected trends and other regularities in the seemingly chaotic hodgepodge of numbers, it formulates a series of hypotheses. Each hypothesis builds upon the previous one, and the process ultimately yields a scientific law.

In one experiment, for example, BACON was asked to consider measurements relating to the solar system. From the data, it hypothesized a direct relationship between the distance of each planet from the sun and the length of the planet's year. After finding further correlations among the numbers, BACON arrived at the following insight: "The ratio of the square of a planet's year-length to the cube of its distance from the sun is the same for all the planets." That happens to be Johannes Kepler's third law of planetary motion. As formulated by the German astronomer nearly four centuries ago — after years of observation instead of the minutes of digital churning required by BACON — it laid the foundation for Isaac Newton's later discovery of the laws of mechanics.

In another experiment, BACON was given the same type of numerical data about chemistry that was available to the English researcher John Dalton in the early 1800s. Because of its ability to determine whether each member of a sequence of measurements is a multiple of some other number, the program rediscovered Dalton's law of multiple proportions, which holds that chemical elements tend to combine with one another in simple, whole-number ratios. That insight led Dalton to postulate a concept fundamental to modern chemistry and physics — the existence of the atom.

Though BACON's talent for discovery — or, more accurately, rediscovery — is impressive, it represents little progress toward the goal of making machine learning less dependent on people. Like Patrick Winston's explorations of learning by example, BACON leaves most of the creative work to the human programmers. They, not the program itself, select the data and decide upon the relevant features or measurements that are fed into the machine.

Similarly, critics argue, BACON is so proficient at discovery only because of the centuries of hard human effort that preceded it. Douglas B. Lenat, a former junior colleague of the program's principal creator, Herb Simon, has pointed out that BACON depends upon precise measurements and carefully honed mathematical techniques developed by generations of scientists since the original discov-

EXAMPLES
ADVICE
DATA

INITIAL KNOWLEDGE

FEEDBACK

Design for a Self-Modifying Machine

Task-specific programs for such applications as word processing, spreadsheets or computer games are designed to perform a particular function in a particular way, by following rules of operation that the program itself cannot change. Even most expert systems *(pages 43-53)* are limited to heuristic rules and a knowledge base supplied by a human authority; they are incapable of adding to this knowledge or of modifying their performance on the basis of experience.

Learning programs, in contrast, are intended to take those extra steps. Already, some programs can simplify scientific research by discerning patterns in unorganized masses of data; more sophisticated machine learning will be necessary for ventures into deep space, where computers aboard spacecraft will require their own investigatory and decision-making capabilities.

The diagram at left represents a synthesis of the elements common to most models of machine learning, whether for programs designed to learn by example, analogy, discovery or instruction *(pages 85-97)*. Central to the model is a core of so-called initial knowledge, illustrated here as a gold mass. As in expert systems, this initial knowledge is supplied by the programmer and includes both heuristics pertaining to the subject, often entered into the program as if-then statements, and facts. Initial knowledge may also include coded instructions for organizing information, as well as metaknowledge, which is sometimes described as the program's awareness of its own strengths and weaknesses.

Machine learning results from the interaction of initial knowledge with various kinds of input and output. Input *(green arrow)* may consist of advice from the user, which the program must interpret and apply, as well as specific instances or examples, from which the program must induce general rules or concepts. As the program processes this information, it can modify the facts and heuristics in its knowledge base; the modification is then reflected in the program's output, or improved task performance *(blue arrow)*. (In some models, improved performance is defined as being able to give more accurate solutions or as finding solutions at a lower cost; in others, it is defined as expansion of the range of problems the machine can handle or as the machine's ability to simplify its own rules to conserve memory.) Finally, the feedback loop *(red arrow)* evaluates the program's performance, comparing results with goals, isolating errors and recommending corrections. Subsequent improvement is denoted here by the shadowy enlargements of the knowledge base.

PERFORMANCE

MODIFIED RULES

eries. "You give BACON pairs of error-free numbers and it comes up with a mathematical expression relating this input to that output," Lenat has noted. "You can call that discovering laws of physics if you want to, but you really have to squint hard to call it that. Certainly, if Kepler had been told which few variables were relevant and had had the perfect data that BACON did, then it would have only taken *him* about an hour to come up with his law."

Lenat, born in 1950, belongs to a generation not afraid to question its mentors or to try new approaches. In the view of some researchers, Lenat's own work in learning by discovery has been extremely promising, perhaps paving the way for expert systems that can solve problems with a minimum of human intervention.

AN ODD PATH TO AI RESEARCH

A native of Philadelphia and something of a mathematics whiz as a youth, Lenat gravitated to computers while still in high school, for eminently practical reasons. His part-time job at nearby Beaver College — cleaning the animal cages in the psychology department — earned him a dollar an hour; he did not mind the rats, he said later, but when geese were added to the menagerie he went looking for a more pleasant environment. Upon learning that a college student was making $1.50 an hour programming the department's minicomputer, Lenat borrowed the computer's operating manuals, taught himself to program in the space of a single weekend and then won the job away by offering to work for 50 cents less.

This new dollar-an-hour job not only beat cleaning cages but also sparked a passion that led seven years later to graduate study in computer science at Stanford. In 1975, Lenat created a discovery-learning program for his doctoral thesis. Like BACON, Lenat's program was best at rediscovering old laws, but in the province of mathematics rather than physical science. Lenat called this pioneering system AM, for Automated Mathematician.

To enable AM to explore the world of elementary set and number theory, Lenat supplied it with 115 definitions of concepts such as equality and operations such as set intersection. He also provided 250 if-then rules to guide its search for more complex concepts. These rules furnished criteria for focusing on particular avenues of exploration. For example, the machine might be instructed as follows: "If some action is found to be useful in a given situation, then try the same action in similar situations."

Probably the most productive heuristics Lenat wrote for AM were the 59 rules that helped the program assess whether or not something was interesting enough to investigate. The criteria included the presence of regularities and similarities in mathematical relationships. For instance, in the course of investigating the previously discovered concept "divisors of," AM found it interesting that some numbers can be divided evenly by only two divisors — themselves and one — thus discovering the concept of prime numbers.

AM proved to be an apt learner. In only a few hours of operation, it progressed from a state of near illiteracy in mathematics to the rediscovery of some 200 of the most important concepts in number theory. It taught itself the concept of squares (numbers that can be expressed as another number multiplied by itself) and even arrived at a hypothesis known as Goldbach's conjecture — that every even number greater than two is the sum of two prime numbers.

Like Arthur Samuel's classic checkers-playing program, AM also demonstrated a

A Robot's Education by Example

Of all the skills that demonstrate human intelligence, the ability to learn is perhaps the one most difficult to explain and to encode in step-by-step programming procedures. Without that ability, machines will never be able to cope with circumstances not precisely foreseen by a human programmer. With it, computers would have the power to modify their behavior and improve their performance through the independent acquisition of new knowledge. Not surprisingly, then, a variety of approaches to the problem of machine learning have been pursued. Learning techniques range from rote memorization to the more sophisticated method of reasoning by analogy. But perhaps the most widely studied approach is learning by example, also known as learning by induction.

A system is said to learn by example if it can draw general conclusions about a given phenomenon by studying specific instances designated as either positive or negative examples of the phenomenon. To that end, the system requires heuristics, or rules of thumb, to guide it in the induction process, instructing the system to notice certain similarities and differences between positive and negative samples.

In learning by example, the system is also given two kinds of assignments: a learning task (forming generalizations, say) and a performance task, which is the activity to be improved by learning. To accomplish either task, the system must have facts about the subject, or domain, in which it will operate, and other rules of thumb that will facilitate its progress through this domain.

Learning by example is illustrated on the following pages with a highly fanciful story of a robot that must learn to distinguish between two kinds of dragons—those willing to give gold away and those that want only to get gold for themselves. By learning to recognize which dragons are greedy and which are generous, the robot becomes more proficient at its performance task: to gather gold to fill a pot at the end of the rainbow. The methods used by the robot can be applied by real-world computers to such tasks as playing chess or distinguishing among diseases with similar symptoms.

Stocking Up on Initial Knowledge

At the core of a learning system is a built-in packet of information that enables the system to begin its performance and learning tasks. This initial knowledge covers three areas: the performance task, the learning task, and the domain in which performance and learning take place. In systems designed to learn by example, the specific instances encountered may prove a given fact or rule to be wrong or incomplete. The system's learning task is thus to refine its initial knowledge or to create new knowledge because of that experience, improving its performance in the process.

As the robot prepares to begin its assignment, it reads a scroll representing the initial knowledge contained in its learning program *(box, right)*. Its instructions are to follow the rainbow, gathering gold from dragons on the way, and fill the pot at the other end. To accomplish this performance task, the robot must also carry out a learning task — to form a concept, or hypothesis, that will let it recognize generous dragons.

The robot whose learning trial is illustrated here receives as its initial knowledge a number of instructions and facts *(box)*: "Follow the rainbow from beginning to end," for example, pertains to the robot's performance task. Its learning task might be paraphrased as: "Learn to recognize generous dragons." Its domain knowledge consists of statements such as "Dragons possess gold" and so-called generalization hierarchies of dragon attributes. The hierarchies organize relevant features in a way that will let the robot make generalizations from encounters with specific dragons. Domain knowledge also includes heuristics, which give a learning system guidance much as a teacher would. If the robot were programmed to learn to play chess instead of to travel the rainbow and encounter dragons, its domain knowledge would include, among other things, the rules of the game, a description of each of the chess pieces and rules of thumb gleaned from human chess players.

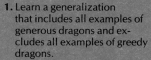

A Starter Kit of Rules and Facts

The list below reveals the different types of initial knowledge built into the robot's program. Item 1 spells out the robot's learning task, and items 2 through 4 list the conditions of the performance task. Items 5 through 8, together with the three generalization hierarchies *(below, right)*, give the robot facts about dragons; item 9 outlines the hypothesis that the robot must form by learning to associate certain features with generous behavior. Finally, the robot is given one heuristic, item 10; without it, the robot would be paralyzed — it would have no basis for approaching its first dragon.

1. Learn a generalization that includes all examples of generous dragons and excludes all examples of greedy dragons.
2. Follow the rainbow from beginning to end.
3. Ask generous dragons for gold; avoid greedy dragons.
4. Fill the pot at the end of the rainbow with gold.
5. Dragons possess gold.
6. Greedy dragons will try to steal gold.
7. Generous dragons will give gold.
8. A dragon may be any shape and any color and may live in any habitat.
9. A generous dragon is (----------) shape, (--------) color and lives in (--------) habitat.
10. Assume a dragon is generous unless you have evidence to the contrary.

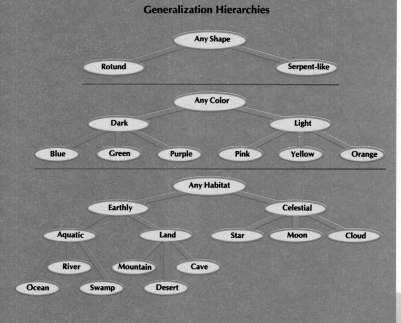

Generalization Hierarchies

A Proliferation of Possibilities

The attributes in the generalization hierarchies that form part of the robot's initial knowledge *(below)* serve as the raw material for the learning task by defining the characteristics deemed relevant. Because the robot has yet to encounter any actual dragons (and because it has no preconceived notions about the attributes necessary to describe generous dragons), it treats all of this information as equally valid in describing generous dragons.

The generalizations the robot makes here — concepts that it holds as hypotheses — thus include all possible combinations of the attributes of shape, color and habitat that the robot has been given. These combinations range from the very broad to the very narrow. For example, the generalization (any shape, any color, any habitat) covers every possible dragon, while (rotund, dark, celestial) covers a smaller subset of the presumed dragon population, and (serpent-like, yellow, river) describes fewer dragons still.

However, not all dragons are generous; if the robot is to accomplish its performance task — to gather gold and fill the pot at the end of the rainbow — it must learn quickly to distinguish generous dragons from greedy ones. As soon as the robot encounters its first dragon, it will begin to winnow this cumbersome mass of concepts by a process of inductive reasoning.

Generalization Hierarchies

The number of hypotheses the robot can form about generous dragons is equal to the number of possible shapes (3) times the number of possible colors (9) times the number of possible habitats (14), for a total of 378. Until the robot encounters its first example of a dragon — (rotund, dark, ocean), say, or (serpent-like, orange, star) — it cannot begin to eliminate any of the possibilities; it must retain all 378 combinations as plausible generalizations of generous dragons.

Rotund
Light
Land

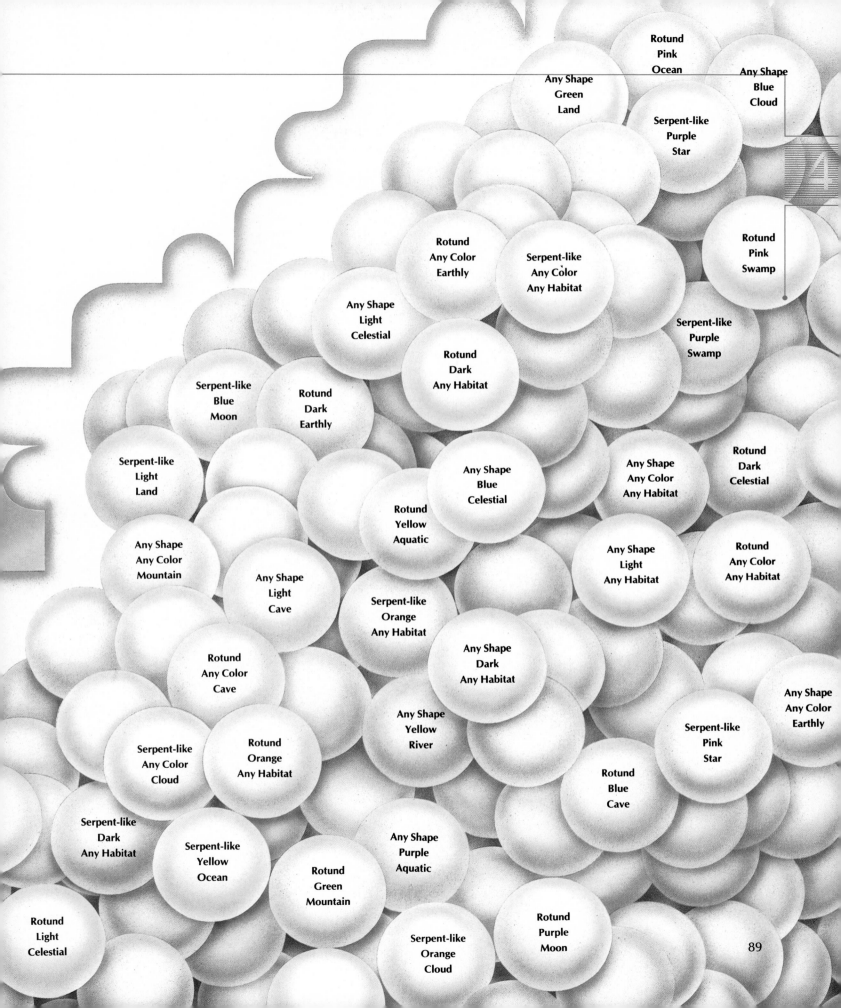

89

Close Encounters: The Learning Begins

As the robot begins its journey, it also begins the process of reducing its 378 possible generalizations down to a single correct one. It approaches its first dragon without hesitation, since it does not yet have evidence that any of the generalizations about generous dragons are false. The first encounter and each succeeding one will act as feedback for the robot's learning program: Each instance of greedy or generous dragon behavior will tell the robot how good its current set of generalizations is, allowing it to refine its knowledge base by eliminating all generalizations that no longer cover the specific examples of generous dragons the robot has encountered.

An AI program designed to learn by example is usually given both positive and negative instances as input, since a learning program that encounters only positive examples may overgeneralize. If a machine-learning system is supposed to learn to recognize dogs, say, but is shown pictures of 10 different breeds and told each time, ''This is a dog,'' it might conclude that all four-legged animals are dogs. Only if it were shown pictures of elephants, cats and other four-legged animals that are not dogs could the system begin to refine its generalization in a meaningful way.

By the same token, the robot on these pages will learn most quickly if it encounters both generous and greedy dragons, even though losing gold to greedy dragons will temporarily hamper its performance task. If a dragon gives the robot gold, the robot will immediately eliminate all generalizations that do not match or include that generous dragon's shape, color and habitat on all counts. If a dragon takes gold away, the robot will eliminate all generalizations that do match or include the attributes of the greedy dragon on all counts. Eventually, the robot will weed out all generalizations but the correct one, which must describe all of the generous — and none of the greedy — dragons the robot has met.

The robot approaches the first dragon — which is rotund and pink and lives in the mountains — asks for gold and receives it. On the basis of this generous behavior, the robot eliminates 354 generalizations, such as (serpent-like, yellow, celestial), that do not match or encompass the dragon's attributes on all counts and therefore cannot be the correct generalization for generous dragons. Only 24 generalizations — ranging from the narrow (rotund, pink, mountain) to the broad (any shape, any color, any habitat) — are still plausible.

Rotund Pink Mountain	Any Shape Pink Mountain	Rotund Light Mountain	Any Shape Light Mountain
Rotund Pink Land	Any Shape Pink Land	Rotund Light Land	Any Shape Light Land
Rotund Pink Earthly	Any Shape Pink Earthly	Rotund Light Earthly	Any Shape Light Earthly
Rotund Pink Any Habitat	Any Shape Pink Any Habitat	Rotund Light Any Habitat	Any Shape Light Any Habitat

Next, the robot approaches a rotund, purple, mountain-dwelling dragon; because the dragon's description fits several of the remaining generalizations about generous dragons, it is possible that this dragon is generous. But instead of giving the robot gold, the dragon snatches some away. On the basis of this greedy behavior, the robot eliminates eight generalizations that describe the first dragon but also describe the second. Only 16 generalizations about generous dragons remain viable.

A Robot's Education by Example

The robot next meets a serpent-like, yellow, swamp-dwelling dragon and asks for gold. (Had the dragon been blue instead of yellow, the robot would have avoided it.) When the beast turns out to be generous, the robot discards all generalizations that do not cover it, leaving only one — (any shape, light, earthly) — which applies to both of the generous dragons the robot has met and to neither of the greedy dragons. If the learning-by-example method is successful, this will be the right generalization, and the robot should easily obtain enough gold to fill the pot at the end of the rainbow.

The next dragon the robot sees is rotund and pink and lives in the stars. Because the dragon fits four of the remaining generalizations, the robot approaches and asks the dragon for gold. This proves to be a mistake: The dragon turns out to be a greedy one. Escaping with its depleted sack of gold, the robot eliminates four more generalizations. Of the remaining 12 generalizations, all fit the one generous dragon the robot has met so far, and none apply to either of the greedy dragons encountered.

Rotund Pink Mountain	Any Shape Pink Mountain	Rotund Light Mountain	Any Shape Light Mountain
Rotund Pink Land	Any Shape Pink Land	Rotund Light Land	Any Shape Light Land
Rotund Pink Earthly	Any Shape Pink Earthly	Rotund Light Earthly	Any Shape Light Earthly

Examining the Final Hypothesis

After encountering four examples, the robot has formed a generalization about generous dragons. Henceforth, it will ask for gold only from dragons covered by the (any-shape, light, earthly) generalization and will avoid all others. However, like any other system that learns by example, the robot runs the risk of having overgeneralized or overspecialized: The robot's generalization may in fact cover some greedy dragons; it may also fail to cover some generous ones.

Overgeneralization and overspecialization can be caused by imperfect, or noisy, data. Perhaps the celestial dragon the robot met is normally generous but was in a bad mood that day. Its greedy behavior would constitute a so-called false-negative sample. Conversely, one of the dragons that behaved generously might be a false positive. Other errors can be introduced by incorrect first assumptions built into the system — that greed and generosity can be judged on the basis of shape, color and habitat, for instance, or that the generalization hierarchy itself is complete. The algorithms employed in machine-learning systems can minimize the risk of these kinds of errors. Often, a generalization can be useful even if it is not valid in all cases: The robot has learned a means of judging which dragons to approach and which to avoid.

Contemplating the two dragons it knows from experience to be generous, the robot is surrounded by images of the many dragons it now assumes, sight unseen, to be generous as well. Their attributes are all covered by the generalization the robot has formed: that generous dragons are any shape, light-colored and live in earthly habitats. Further experience may cause the robot to modify the generalization — provided it is programmed with that capacity — but for now it will continue to seek gold of any dragon on the path that meets this description.

Other Paths to the Same Goal

Having made a viable generalization about generous dragons, the robot is ready to complete its performance task by filling the pot at the end of the rainbow with gold. Other machine-learning techniques could have been employed as well, albeit with varying results. The robot could have learned by rote, for instance, simply memorizing the description and behavior of each dragon it encountered. This unsophisticated method would be useful only if the robot met the same dragon more than once.

Learning by instruction would have involved storing great

EXAMPLE

ROTE

ANALOGY

quantities of information about dragon lore in the robot's memory and programming the machine to find logical patterns of greedy and generous dragon behavior. Learning by analogy would have been possible only if the robot had come to its learning task with prior knowledge of some similar subject. If the robot had already learned about greedy and generous wizards, say, that knowledge might have been applied to the study of dragons.

One of the most sophisticated machine-learning techniques — and one that is on the frontier of AI research — is learning by discovery. This method involves the open-ended exploration of a subject; no particular learning or performance tasks are specified. Learning by discovery would not have been appropriate for the robot because that method would not have helped the robot collect gold to fill the pot at the end of the rainbow. In any case, learning by discovery requires the ability to draw inferences, recognize patterns, form and test theories, and work with inconclusive data. All are skills at which the human mind is adept but which are not easily written into a computer program.

DISCOVERY

INSTRUCTION

Seeing and Foreseeing

Despite its relative youth, the field of artificial intelligence has already generated its share of folklore. According to one oft-told tale, sometime in the 1960s AI pioneer Marvin Minsky summoned an M.I.T. freshman and blithely gave him a project to complete over the summer. The student's assignment: to study and solve the problem of machine vision. Such an undertaking might have sounded straightforward enough at the time. Most AI researchers were preoccupied with things that, in humans, require rigorous mental effort — symbol-manipulating tasks involving logic, if-then rules or board games. The majority of workers in the field seemed almost to look down on the human sensory and motor skills of seeing, hearing, feeling, grasping and locomotion. These activities, they felt, had little or nothing to do with genuine intelligence. Human vision, for example, occurs instantly and without readily discernible thought.

As the hapless student of AI legend soon learned, however, replicating vision in a machine is a problem that does not yield to easy solutions. For that matter, artificial-intelligence researchers have yet to develop a machine that can approach the sensory and motor abilities of even a lowly mosquito as it flies, feeds, breeds and otherwise copes with a complex, constantly changing environment.

Closing the considerable gap in processing power between computers and living creatures is crucial if advances in machine intelligence are ever to occur. Any intelligence, whether natural or artificial, must be able to deal with the real world, a world that consists, for the most part, of often ambiguous physical phenomena rather than precise symbols and logic. Thus, one of the highest priorities of AI research is to devise new methods and hardware to enable machines not only to see, hear and feel but to make sense of their perceptions. A seeing-eye computer system designed to spot certain jungle beasts, for example, would have to be fitted with cameras and programmed with descriptions of the animals it was to identify. Then the system would need to be programmed with such concepts as largeness, grayness and four-leggedness — and be told what animal those characteristics described — in order for it to recognize an elephant.

Although programs that enable computers to see and hear have been improving for decades, the translation of sensory data into concepts remains cumbersome and costly. Some machines used in manufacturing can recognize the silhouette of a specific part moving along a well-lighted assembly line. Workaday home computers fitted with microphones and other hardware and software can, on oral command, turn on lights, dial telephones or even deliver a spoken response. But all such systems are rigidly specialized; they can perceive only single objects outlined against bare, brightly illuminated backgrounds, or recognize small vocabularies of stock words or simple phrases.

No commercially available machine, for instance, can fully comprehend the fabric of sounds that constitutes real-life speech. In contending with actual speech patterns, the computer confronts all the challenges of a written language, compounded by problems of different speaking voices and the way people run

Despite the best efforts of computer scientists, the creation of an artificial intelligence that even approaches the human level remains a goal as remote as the stars; AI awaits discoveries that will open new windows onto the broad realms of human thought.

their words together. The pronunciation of one word often affects the sound of the next. (Did someone say "this story" or "this Tory"?) In practice, the number of possible sound patterns in ordinary speech might as well be infinite.

People, it appears, rely on many kinds of knowledge and many sources of information to carry on cogent conversations. During a crowded, noisy cocktail party, for example, a listener will recognize snatches of talk and then try to predict or hypothesize about the rest, based on the context. A listener straining to hear above the din applies what he or she knows about the speaker and the subject at hand, occasionally critiquing what is being said by asking, in effect, "Can that really be what I heard?" AI experts recognize that any speech-understanding machine will probably have to do likewise.

THE INFANT STAGE OF SPEECH RECOGNITION

In the 1950s, scientists at Bell Laboratories attempted to construct machines that could comprehend speech — or at least recognize and respond to specific sounds — in an effort to permit callers to speak desired telephone numbers into a receiver rather than dialing them. The Bell researchers fell far short of their goal, however, and soon moved on to more achievable projects. Other workers in the field built some rudimentary speech-recognition systems during the 1960s. Among them was a Stanford University graduate student named Raj Reddy, who had come to the United States from a village in rural India. His original specialty had been numerical analysis, which involves using computers to find the solutions to large mathematical problems, but he developed a deep interest in artificial intelligence. It never occurred to him, he recalled later, that AI could not be attained. "That may be exactly what's needed for anybody who wants to go into this field," Reddy said, "namely, blind optimism with no reasonable basis for it."

Reddy's efforts at machine speech recognition barely rose above the baby-talk stage, but he refused to be discouraged. By 1970, he had moved east from Stanford to Carnegie-Mellon University, where, in 1971, he and a number of AI colleagues convened to discuss the qualities that would be needed in a workable system of machine speech recognition. The session was chaired by Allen Newell, whose groundbreaking work with Herbert Simon and J. C. Shaw on Logic Theorist and General Problem Solver had done so much to energize the artificial-intelligence community more than a decade earlier. The sponsor was the Defense Department's Advanced Research Projects Agency (DARPA), which since the 1960s has provided much of the financial support for computer science in general and AI research in particular. Out of this conclave of experts came a five-year, $15 million project, underwritten by DARPA and dubbed SUR — for Speech Understanding Research. The goals were carefully spelled out: to demonstrate the capacity to comprehend around 90 percent of ordinary, continuous speech (as opposed to isolated words) about some limited subject matter, using a vocabulary of at least 1,000 words. Ultimately, several organizations submitted programs, but only two of them — both produced by teams from Carnegie-Mellon headed by Raj Reddy — would meet DARPA's goals.

One of the successful programs was called Hearsay II, after an earlier version. Though limited to answering questions about document retrieval from a collection of computer-science abstracts, Hearsay II was a major advance over Reddy's fledgling efforts at Stanford in the 1960s. The new program was endowed with 12 subprograms to sort out and coordinate different types of information contained in a speech signal. Some of the subprograms specialized in phonetics and phonemics — that is, representations of speech sounds and the rules describing the components that make up speech in a given language. Another specialized in prosodics, or rules for interpreting variations in stress and intonation; still another was concerned with morphemics, or rules for word variations such as plurals or verb conjugations. A syntax subprogram dealt with rules of acceptable sentence formation; a semantic subprogram contended with word meanings. Another subprogram dealt with pragmatics — idioms and the unwritten rules of discourse; this program recognized, for example, that the query, "Can you tell me what time it is?" is commonly understood to require more than a yes-or-no response.

Each of Hearsay II's specialists dealt successively with only small portions of a sentence — a few words or a clause, perhaps. Each subprogram posted its hypothesis about what it thought it heard on a "blackboard," a central repository in memory. Other subprograms could then consult the blackboard to see which hypothesis seemed most plausible. For example, the subprogram for phonetics might think it had heard a certain combination of phonemes. Then a syntax module would weigh in with an opinion about whether such a word was likely to occur at such a place in a sentence.

The innovations that Reddy and his associates built into Hearsay II — multiple

knowledge sources, the blackboard, and the alternation between sensory data and informed expectations — have since become standard in many other AI applications. These techniques have been particularly useful in the daunting field of machine vision; apparently, separating a visual object from its confusing background and identifying it — things that humans and lower animals perform automatically in a fraction of a second — require at least as many different kinds of knowledge as does understanding a spoken sentence.

Meeting the challenges of sensory perception could lead to any number of invaluable applications, such as machines that could convert spoken words into neatly typed pages and vice versa. A vision system able to recognize objects would be well on the way to being autonomous, provided it was also equipped to learn from its environment. But because so much of human perception and learning takes place below the level of consciousness, researchers are faced with the seemingly insurmountable task of trying to program machines to simulate skills that the researchers themselves cannot explain.

Yet even if AI workers knew precisely how to write the programs for machine learning and sensory perception, conventional computers are unlikely ever to be as fast as people at certain kinds of mental processes. Merely to interpret a single scene, for example, the human visual system employs perhaps 10 billion brain cells that each perform a billion large-number calculations every tenth of a second. This is several times the speed of the fastest commercial supercomputers.

Most computers still operate on principles laid out during World War II by mathematician John von Neumann. Designed for sequential calculations with numbers, von Neumann-style computers have banks of memory cells, each capable of containing one or a few symbols, called bits, bytes or words, depending on their size. These cells feed their contents one symbol at a time into a single central processing unit, or CPU. The CPU adds, subtracts, or otherwise combines the symbols one after another and returns the results to memory.

TRAFFIC JAM ON THE DATA BUS

For many potential AI applications, particularly those involving sensory perception and timely responses to real-world events, such computers operate too slowly to be useful. They are inherently limited by what IBM computer scientist John Backus — who headed the team that developed the widely used programming language FORTRAN — has identified as the "von Neumann bottleneck": the lone channel between the CPU and its memory along which data and instructions flow sequentially. The more elements a program has to deal with — in the form of pieces of data and the number and type of operations to be performed — the longer it takes to find a solution, because every piece of information must travel back and forth between memory and CPU as the computer performs its operations one at a time.

The nature of serial computers creates a paradox, as Scott Fahlman pointed out in the late 1970s, while a graduate student in Marvin Minsky's department at M.I.T. In the matter of perception, the more identifying features an object has, the harder it becomes for the computer to achieve a quick recognition, because the machine must work through all the possibilities introduced by each feature. By contrast, humans seem to find that the more distinguishing features an object has, the easier it is to identify. To Fahlman, who moved to Carnegie-Mellon as a research scientist after finishing his studies at M.I.T., this suggests a fundamental difference in the way people go about identifying things. "There are two kinds of thinking," he has said. "There's ordinary linear thinking, like solving an arithmetic problem, and that's modeled well on a serial machine. Then there's recognition — having the right fact pop into your head to deal with a problem. It's very awkward to get that to happen on a serial machine."

Unfortunately for researchers using serial machines, most human mental activity — recognizing and reasoning about patterns, making snap judgments, associations, generalizations, analogies and the like — seems to be the largely unconscious product of this second kind of thinking. Presumably, no serial computer will ever be able to sort through such an array of information as quickly as the data would be needed by, say, an autonomous robot explorer. Spying a large, gray, four-legged shape with big ears trotting down a jungle path, the robot would be at a dangerous disadvantage if it had to find and combine lists of properties in serial fashion before deciding that it was about to be trampled by an elephant.

Besides having difficulty with object recognition, computers of whatever type also cannot deal readily with such things as time, cause and effect, and so-called fuzzy concepts, which lack precise or constant meaning. One example of a fuzzy concept is the word "far": Depending on the context, people readily accept that "far" can refer to anything from atomic-scale to galactic-scale distances. Designing a program that allows a computer to operate on vague rules and imprecise definitions is one of the central challenges of AI.

RADICAL DESIGNS FOR AMBITIOUS GOALS

Given the complexity of AI problems, most researchers in the early 1980s had concluded that any machine intelligence worthy of the name probably needed new types of computers. Japan's widely publicized Fifth-Generation Computer Project, launched in 1982, was based on some emerging ideas for non-von Neumann machines. The stated goal of this ambitious undertaking is to build computers that operate several thousand times more rapidly than do the fastest von Neumann machines, and to devise software that will allow these advanced computers to understand spoken and written language, to learn, to reason and, in general, to perform most tasks that require human intelligence.

The principal idea behind this and other such efforts is called parallel processing (pages 104-107). By dividing the processing labor among many small devices, such as inexpensive silicon chips, parallelism offers the hope of quantum leaps in processing power at low cost. Perhaps the main attraction of this approach is that it mimics nature itself. While a single electronic computer processor operates thousands of times more rapidly than does its individual neuron equivalent, networks of neurons perform many kinds of tasks, especially nonnumerical ones, thousands of times more rapidly than computers. This is because the neurons are linked together in such a way that individual neurons can solve different problems or perform separate sensory and motor functions simultaneously — in parallel rather than serially.

So bright are the promises of electronic parallel processing that some researchers have even revived the ideas of the cyberneticists — bottom-up analyses of signal patterns and learning, using networks of simulated neurons. These efforts were spurred greatly in the early 1980s by publication of a book titled *Parallel*

The Limitations of a Serial Machine

Despite advances in computer technology — from vacuum tubes to transistors to integrated circuits and, most recently, to very-large-scale integrated (VLSI) circuits — computers have scarcely changed at all in one respect: Most are still so-called serial machines, operating on principles defined by mathematician and computer pioneer John von Neumann in the mid-1940s. Von Neumann architecture ensures a flexible general-purpose computer, but it has one critical flaw: Machines of this design can carry out only one operation at a time, a limitation that has driven computer engineers to search for speedier alternatives (pages 102-108).

As shown conceptually below, a serial computer consists of a central processing unit (CPU), which directs operations and performs calculations; a memory, which holds instructions and data pertaining to the current program; and an electronic pathway between the two called a data bus. To execute a simple operation such as adding two numbers, most computers must take several steps, each of which requires moving data on the data bus. Because the bus can accommodate only one instruction or piece of data at a time, however, the steps must be done one after another; if many calculations are involved, the data bus becomes a significant bottleneck.

Most problems in artificial intelligence are too large or complicated to be handled in this fashion. No matter how fast the CPU can perform operations, the time spent shuttling information back and forth across the data bus is so great that the machine cannot solve a problem quickly enough for the solution to be useful. For instance, one experimental mobile AI-vision system hooked up to a powerful serial computer processes information from a digitized image consisting of a quarter million picture elements, or pixels. Although it uses a sophisticated algorithm to filter out all but the most relevant data, the device can negotiate a small obstacle course only by stopping for one minute every yard or so to recompute its own position and those of nearby obstacles.

The grid at right represents the brightness value of each pixel in one area of the digitized image of the hammer. In a machine-vision system *(pages 14-29)*, a preliminary step of edge detection, called smoothing, involves manipulating brightness values to get rid of minor fluctuations in intensity. Here, each pixel's value will be replaced with an average of its four neighbors'. To perform this step for the pixels in a 512-by-480-pixel image, a fast serial computer needs about three seconds; it would then take about seven minutes for the machine to perform a full edge detection on the image.

66	76	70	71	76	74
48	55	60	69	71	75
52		63	71	70	75
			68	67	78
	49			65	72
			45		70

Parallelism: A Strategy for Speed

In an attempt to break the so-called von Neumann bottleneck of serial processing, scientists have experimented with radically different computer designs, all of which fall under the rubric of parallel processing, a scheme that allows multiple calculations to be performed simultaneously. The illustration below depicts one possible configuration of a so-called massively parallel computer; this machine would be composed of hundreds of thousands of small processors *(white)*, each equipped with its own memory *(dark blue)*.

With such an arrangement, edge detection on the 512-by-480-pixel image described on the preceding page could be done in a fraction of the time it would take on a serial machine. Instead of performing the calculations sequentially, this computer could put 245,760 processors to work

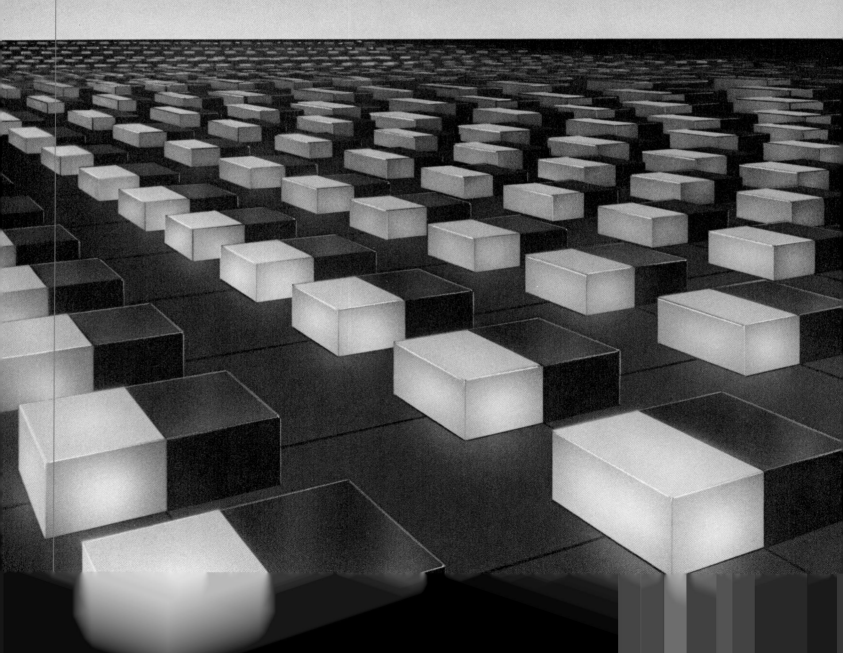

simultaneously, one per pixel. Each processor would communicate its own value to each of its four neighbors, receiving a value from each in turn and keeping a running total in its own memory; a processor would then divide its total by four to get the new value for its pixel. Instead of taking three seconds to compute the new values for 245,760 pixels, the processors could complete the necessary calculations in about half a millisecond — 6,000 times faster than a fast serial machine.

Such phenomenal increases in speed will certainly be a boon to the development of machine vision, but building computers with more than one processor raises many design questions. For example: Should processors be relatively few but large and powerful, or small and simple but many thou- sands in number? Should overall control reside in a master control unit, represented here as the large structure visible on the horizon, or be dispersed somehow among several (or several hundred thousand) processors? Should each processor have its own memory or should there be a common memory for all — and if so, what happens when two processors want the same piece of data at the same time? The physical wiring of so many components also becomes problematic, to say nothing of figuring out how to write programs for parallel machines. Ultimately, different designs may be deemed appropriate for different types of problems, just as the allocation of human labor varies with the particular task at hand: Painting a fence lends itself to the kind of parallelism useful in machine vision; painting a work of art does not.

Models of Associative Memory, a collection of papers jointly edited by Geoffrey Hinton, a young Englishman who studied AI, psychology and neurophysiology at the University of Edinburgh before joining the Carnegie-Mellon faculty, and James Anderson, a neurophysiologist at Brown University. Hinton, Anderson and their contributing authors laid out persuasive arguments that so-called massively parallel computers — modeled on neuron networks — would be far better at many functions of intelligence than von Neumann computers.

The difference in capabilities between biological information-processing systems and serial computers begins at the most basic physical levels. For one thing, memory in neuron networks is thought to be distributed throughout the structure, not localized at a particular place as it is in serial machines. Moreover, in biological networks, memory usually takes the form of strengthened or weakened connections between neurons rather than of stored binary symbols. Scientists believe that either through innate properties or through learning, biology's networks are, in effect, tuned to respond to specific stimuli. It is possible, for example, that every person learns to construct "elephant detectors" that are activated by the right combination of features such as largeness, grayness and four-leggedness.

In such distributed memories, each neuron is simultaneously its own decision maker and its own store of memory. One advantage of this arrangement is resilience: Damage to a few neurons does not radically alter stored data or shut down the whole system, as does cutting a wire or damaging a single transistor in a serial computer. A more important characteristic of distributed memory systems is their potential for what AI workers call content addressability. Instead of being assigned to a memory cell with an arbitrary numerical address, each piece of information in a distributed memory is filed and retrieved according to its content. People do something similar to reconstruct their detailed knowledge when it is needed. Asked what she ate for lunch on the previous Friday, for example, a child might proceed by trying to recall various things that happened that day, especially around lunchtime, which may in turn remind her of what she ate.

HUMAN TRICKS OF ASSOCIATION

Associations like these seem to underlie most human thought: We recall things from partial knowledge, by reminders from similar concepts, even by deliberate associative tricks such as the proverbial piece of string tied around a finger. People do not even add numbers in the purely mechanical way that computers do; instead we associate memorized phrases like "two plus two" with the word "four." Such associations, laborious and time-consuming for serial computers but swift in a distributed memory, also probably lie at the heart of human perception, recognition, generalization, learning and intuition.

It may be that the thinking process is a matter of "spreading activation," a kind of chain reaction in which activity in one network stimulates associated responses in others. The ability to perceive both time and cause and effect, so difficult for computers, may be built into neuron operations and therefore be fundamental to the thinking process. Even very primitive types of learning depend critically on the sequence and timing of events. In habituation, for instance, animals learn to ignore repeated but unimportant stimuli, such as the ticking of a clock, thus freeing up mental resources for more important matters. Sensitization is the opposite: It strengthens responses to stimuli that have important consequences, such as the screech of a braking automobile.

A new school of machine-intelligence researchers—whose adherents call themselves the new connectionists because they see thinking as mainly involving neuron-like connections rather than symbols—argues that if computers are to behave more like brains, they will have to look more like brains. In essence, they call for devices that—much like Frank Rosenblatt's perceptrons of the 1950s and 1960s—consist of intricately linked simulations of neurons.

The connectionist and content-addressable schemes have certain flaws; given their free-form organization, they have the potential to confuse different pieces of data. But equally free-form processes such as habituation, sensitization and association seem to underlie human psychological idiosyncrasies, and Yale's Roger Schank speculates that these idiosyncrasies will have to be incorporated in any computer with pretensions to intelligence. Schank, a leader in the push for machines that can understand natural language, has said: "Today's computers can read the same newspaper story dozens of times and never realize it; they just learn the same stuff all over again. Machines won't become intelligent until they are capable of being bored by something old or surprised by something new."

COMPUTERS THAT MAKE CONNECTIONS

Many researchers hope that parallel-processing machines will achieve this state. Scientists have embarked on several projects to create devices that will be able to learn—through exploration, observation, and trial and error—to do things not easily taught by any programmer.

One of the more ambitious such projects has been developed by the optimistically named Thinking Machines Corporation, a small company in Cambridge, Massachusetts. This processor was conceived by Daniel Hillis while he was still studying robotics at M.I.T. under Marvin Minsky. A native of Oklahoma, Hillis has a taste for unconventional transportation; he has been known to drive a secondhand fire engine. He has also enjoyed broad acquaintance among the clowns of the Ringling Brothers and Barnum & Bailey Circus. More than once, the citizens of Boston have been startled by the sight of Hillis and his clown friends aboard the fire engine, racing about the city with sirens hooting and bells ringing.

In 1985, the first Connection Machine system was completed, with 65,000 processors and memories working in concert. Ultimately, Hillis' machine might consist of a million or more processors, each roughly equivalent in power to the processor in a home computer and each possessing its own memory. Hillis' main innovation is the machine's elaborate and flexible system of interconnections and switches that let processors broadcast information and requests for help to all other processors, simulating brainlike associative recall. The system also permits users to rearrange these interconnections through programming and thus, in effect, construct different parallel computers tailored to applications that might range from making medical diagnoses to operating a robot vehicle.

A similar project is the so-called Boltzmann machine, a concept developed at Carnegie-Mellon by Geoffrey Hinton, Scott Fahlman, Terrence J. Sejnowsky of Johns Hopkins University and other researchers. (The machine is named after Ludwig Boltzmann, one of the 19th-century founders of the statistically based science of thermodynamics.) As in neuron networks, memory in the Boltzmann machine would consist largely of patterns of interconnections rather than symbols stored in specific memory cells. In operation, a Boltzmann machine would attempt to match input patterns with stored patterns of connections.

A sobering fact of life for neural modelers—much of whose work has been limited to simulations on serial computers—is that in the animal kingdom, the differences in intelligence among species seem at least roughly proportional to the number of neurons in the brains of members of each species. Building workable parallel computers with the billions of processors needed to approximate the 100 billion neurons in a human brain will require considerable ingenuity.

Many new connectionists do seem to acknowledge that insights from more traditional approaches to AI research may help meet this challenge. For example, logic and symbol processing could augment connectionism, just as they have augmented human thought through such inventions as mathematics. Marvin Minsky, for one, envisions a combined effort in which many parallel, perceptron-like machines deal mainly with the real world, translating sensory data into symbolic forms for more traditional computers to manipulate.

The drive to achieve machine intelligence must rank as one of the most extraordinary of human undertakings. And the short history of that quest has only increased the respect that most of the participants have for the power and resources of the human brain. Given the present approaches and concepts, realizing the dream of a machine with general-purpose, human-grade intelligence will take formidable advances in hardware and software—many millions of processors and many millions of rules and facts. All that raises doubts about whether such a prospect is in fact realistic. Some, such as Carnegie-Mellon robotics expert Hans Moravec, think that it is. In Moravec's view, the secret lies mainly in building faster computers, either through parallelism or by some other means. Indeed, he believes that the goal of human-level intelligence could be attained quite early in the 21st century. But such optimism is not shared by many.

To be sure, AI's dogged pursuit of its ambitious goals continues to influence all of computer technology; it is no longer easy even to distinguish AI from the rest of computer research. But not all AI workers find cause to rejoice in this acceptance by the scientific mainstream. In fact, the field has a two-edged saying that is part admission and part complaint: "If it's useful, it isn't AI." Traditionally, AI has attracted the kind of people most inclined to chase receding horizons, scientists who give little thought to the practical applications of their work; as soon as some perplexing facet of human intelligence is reduced to workaday engineering practice, it loses its mystery and appeal for dedicated AI researchers. As Marvin Minsky has observed: "When you explain something, you explain it away."

Perhaps so, but human intelligence is far from having been stripped of its mystery. Centuries may pass before science devises machines that have the range, versatility and general ingenuity of the average educated person, much less of a genius. In the short run, many powerful and useful AI products will emerge to handle narrow realms of expertise and special-purpose sensory and mobility tasks; particularly useful to ordinary people will be systems that can communicate knowledge in everyday language. But for the foreseeable future, computers will probably remain what machines have always been—aids for specialized jobs. For at least another century, the generalists—the dreamers and schemers, the problem posers and problem solvers—will still be people, relying on their peerless biological brains.

The Space Frontier

Through persistent and often brilliant efforts over more than three decades, researchers in various scientific disciplines have managed to fill in a few of the pieces of the very large puzzle that is artificial intelligence. Some of those pieces — notably expert systems, computer vision, automation and robotics, and programs for natural-language comprehension — have yielded immediate practical applications in such fields as business, medicine, and the automobile and oil industries.

But among the endeavors that stand to gain from further progress in AI, space exploration may well be the biggest beneficiary. In recent years, the National Aeronautics and Space Administration (NASA), the U.S. Department of Defense and various commercial aerospace companies have all accelerated investigation into those areas of AI that hold out the most promise for achieving an ambitious goal: the creation of computer systems that can serve as human surrogates in space.

The machines that ultimately result from this research must all be capable of acting with some degree of autonomy. At a minimum, these systems will need knowledge bases, whether of a general or a specialized nature, and a means of drawing upon that knowledge to make inferences and judgments. Some machines will require the ability to navigate through space, others to make their way on the surfaces of distant planets or moons. And to be as versatile and useful as possible, of course, these computerized explorers should possess not only sensory faculties such as vision, hearing and touch but also the capacity to learn from experience.

Some aspect of each of these abilities has been pioneered (with widely varying success) in a number of different earthbound machines, and an expert system called LES (for Liquid Oxygen Expert System) has been tested for use with the space shuttle. Given what has been done and what is being studied, the illustrations on the following pages represent one scenario for some of the ways computers equipped with artificial intelligence might be put to work in space sometime in the 21st century. Still, this kind of extrapolation is risky business at best; as one observer has put it, "The paradox of predicting the sciences is that to know what will be known in the future is to have the knowledge today."

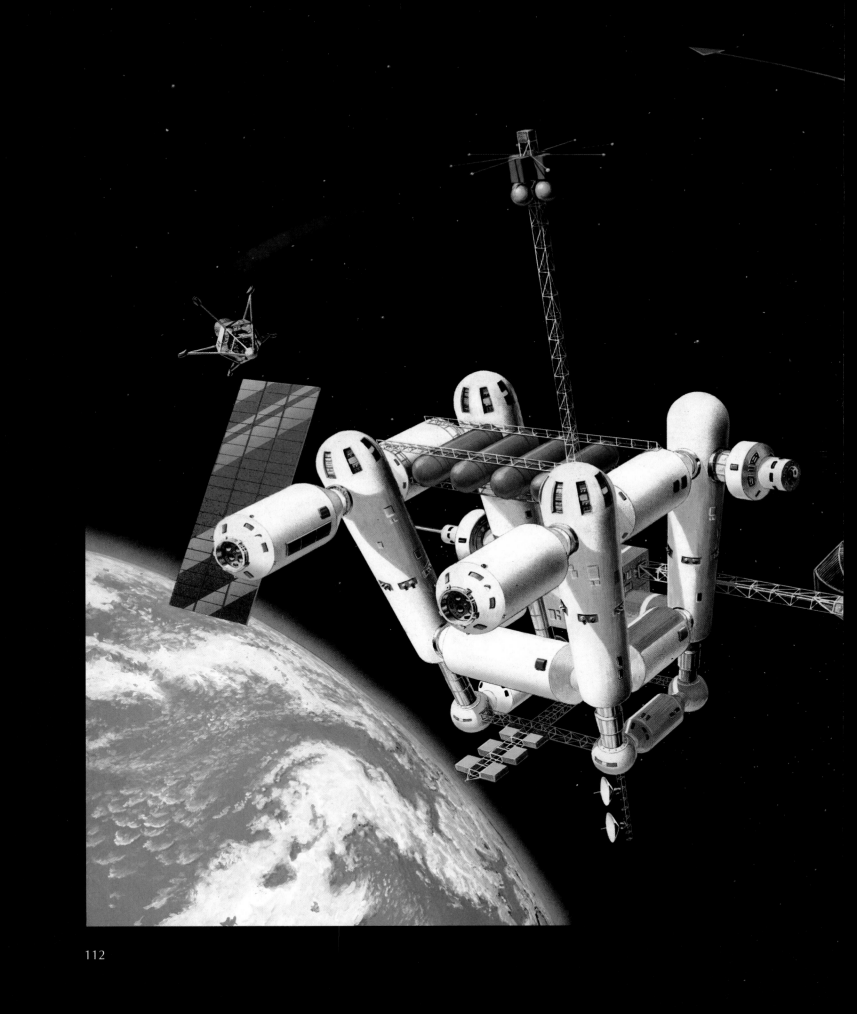

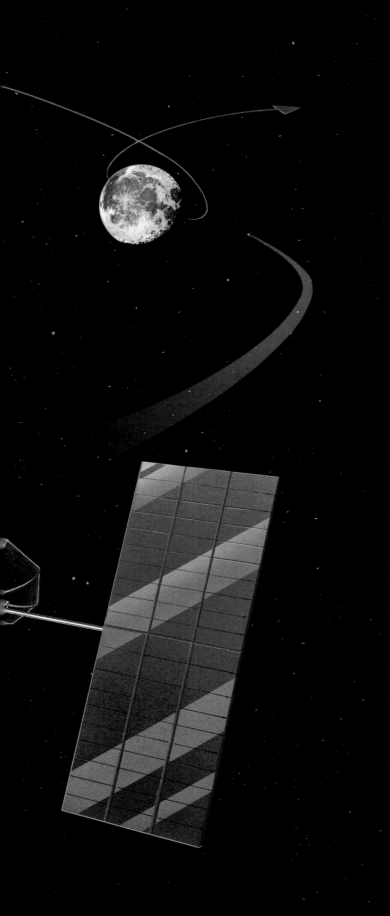

An Automated Depot

Earth's first permanent outpost in space, scheduled for completion by the mid-1990s, will be stationed 250 miles above the earth's surface in LEO, or Lower Earth Orbit. The multipurpose research-and-manufacturing facility will be constructed with so-called hooks and scars — entry points built into computer software and hardware that will allow new AI technology to be integrated as it develops during the station's expected 15- to 20-year life span.

This evolutionary process has been likened to the gradual creation of an electronic colleague for the station's human crew. Unlike robot characters in the movies, the space station's AI component probably will not possess human physical characteristics. Initially at least, it is more likely to consist of a large collection of expert systems principally devoted to monitoring and regulating the station's internal environment and external physical condition. The technology for this will derive in part from some experimental ground-based systems being developed for the space program. Among such systems are KATE (for Knowledge-Based Automatic Test Equipment), a sophisticated troubleshooter that can control hardware as well as monitor it, and IMIS, an Intelligent Management Information System that retrieves information from a data base and answers queries in easy-to-understand language. The space station will possess an array of sensors, including video cameras equipped with pattern-recognition software, that will watch over the station's power, environmental-control and life-support systems. Anomalies or unusual trends will be evaluated by rule-based inference systems and explained to human crew members in natural language and through graphic displays.

As its systems evolve, the space station will reach a kind of adolescence. In this intermediate phase, the station's AI component will achieve moderate autonomy, based partly on the development of natural-language programs that allow the system to respond to spoken queries and partly on visual and tactile sensors that enhance its monitoring abilities. Perhaps at this stage, the station-wide system will develop basic learning skills. With the advent of more sophisticated software, it could, for example, respond to an emergency not precisely covered by its expert systems — it might recognize similarities between the new problem and a situation that is treated in its knowledge base and modify its solution accordingly.

Like a celestial bus depot, the space station will eventually serve as home base to a fleet of autonomous vehicles. Machine-vision and rule-based navigational systems will give these extraterrestrial workhorses the skills to find their own way to and from the moon and to carry out such chores as locating and retrieving satellites for servicing.

Home Base for a Robot Force

The geometric array of structures at right is an artist's rendition of a 21st-century autonomous facility for research and the processing of mineral resources on the moon. According to one scheme, a seed community of robots armed with a starter kit of manufacturing equipment could construct such a facility out of lunar materials and operate it with minimal human supervision. The technology could eventually be employed on more distant bases, such as the Martian moons of Phobos and Deimos and on Mars itself.

This ambitious plan stems in part from a welter of proposals for so-called self-replicating systems, automata that can build their own offspring, which can duplicate themselves in turn. In the first phase of lunar development, this method would be used to create a large force of robot prospectors, miners and factory workers.

Easier to maintain on the moon's inhospitable surface than humans would be, these mechanical natives would construct a solar-powered factory where elements such as iron, titanium, aluminum, silicon and oxygen could be extracted from lunar soil. These would then be fashioned into various products, such as spacecraft parts, that could be used on the moon or exported to the space station or to zero-gravity assembly plants in LEO.

The notion of robots capable of building and operating factories — and of reproducing themselves as well — suggests the achievement of the kind of broad-gauge machine intelligence that has long been the goal of AI research. In fact, however, the robots envisioned for space exploration in the early part of the 21st century will probably be advanced versions of the domain-specific, rule-based expert systems that exist today. These systems will likely be equipped with the lightning-fast processors expected to result from research into parallel-computer architecture *(pages 102-108)*. With additional increases in power, later systems will be orders of magnitude more adept than their predecessors at processing huge quantities of data from visual and tactile sensors and at manipulating the complex rules and knowledge bases that allow the systems to operate without on-site human guidance. The more subtle and elusive qualities of human intelligence — including the ability to learn from experience and to modify behavior accordingly — will probably remain on the frontiers of AI research during the first decades of these pioneering communities.

A versatile transport vehicle passes above a lunar research-and-manufacturing facility built out of raw materials from nearby open-pit mines. Manufactured products, such as spaceship components made from aluminum, could be sent off to destinations such as the zero-gravity assembly plant faintly visible in the sky.

The Advance Team on Distant Worlds

The autonomy of machines in space is likely to range from the limited freedom of devices aboard the space station to the greater independence of a host of orbital and planetary vehicles capable of operating for extended periods without direct human intervention. Continued improvement in certain major areas of AI and robotic research — vision and other sensing systems, for example, and systems that enable robots to manipulate various objects — should give these machines near-human precision and dexterity.

Land-based rovers similar to the explorer illustrated at right represent an advanced stage of robotic development. Designed for the systematic investigation of the surface of the moon and Mars, the rovers will incorporate technological advances tested first in machines used aboard the space station. There, devices will initially work under the close supervision of humans, who will manipulate them by remote control, virtually joint by joint. Eventually, with the addition of pattern-recognition systems and more extensive knowledge bases, robots will have the capacity to carry out simple maintenance chores in and around the station. Developments in tactile sensors and in the control of manipulator arms (already begun on earth with robot arms used to aid surgeons in the operating room) will give robots aboard the space station the ability to perform delicate scientific experiments and precision manufacturing chores in the onboard labs and commercial plants.

All such improvements — and more besides — will be needed to deploy autonomous spacecraft and land-based machines on unsupervised missions. Unmanned land vehicles will have to be equipped with cores of information and rules of thumb for planetary exploration. The robot rovers will also need to possess highly developed vision systems, employing color-television cameras, laser-based radar and pattern-recognition software. These vision systems will also require high-speed processors to allow the machines to deal with visual data as rapidly as it comes in. As dexterous as their predecessors in the space station's labs, the rovers will go to work gathering soil and other samples while negotiating around the boulders and craters of unmapped territories.

A six-wheeled planetary rover, modeled after a prototype autonomous land vehicle developed for military reconnaissance missions, scouts the surface of Mars for mineral resources, water and possible settlement sites. Tactile sensors probe the ground ahead and flexible arms gather soil samples while stereo cameras relay visual information to the rover's vision system.

In the 21st century, robot explorers may roam the universe, relaying news about life in other galaxies.

Glossary

Algorithm: a method or procedure for solving a problem.

Analog: the representation of a continuously changing physical variable (temperature, for example) by another physical variable (such as the height of a column of mercury).

Analog electronic simulation: a method of simulating intelligence by use of a machine with components that directly represent neurons; *see* Bottom-up theory.

Analogy learning: the process of acquiring new knowledge or skills by applying similar existing knowledge to a new situation.

Arithmetic logic unit: a part of the central processor that performs arithmetic operations such as subtraction and logical operations such as TRUE-FALSE comparisons.

Artificial intelligence (AI): the ability of a machine to perform functions normally associated with human intelligence, such as comprehending spoken language, making judgments and learning.

Automatic feedback control: the use of information from the outside world to correct a machine's behavior.

Autonomous: capable of independent action.

Binary number system: a number system that uses two as its base and expresses numbers as strings of zeros and ones.

Bit: the smallest unit of information in a binary computer, represented by a single zero or one. The word "bit" is a contraction of "binary digit."

Bottom-up theory: an approach to artificial intelligence aimed at mechanically duplicating the human brain to create adaptive networks.

Byte: a sequence of bits, usually eight, treated as a unit for computation or storage.

Central processing unit (CPU): the part of a computer that interprets and executes instructions. It is composed of an arithmetic logic unit, a control unit and a small amount of memory.

Combinatorial explosion: the exponential growth in the number of possible choices in a problem-solving search.

Computer architecture: the internal layout, or design, of a computer.

Computer vision: *see* Machine vision.

Conceptual dependency: a theory of language comprehension maintaining that people mentally translate all language into underlying conceptual structures.

Content addressability: a method of storing information in which data is filed and retrieved according to its content rather than by an arbitrary numerical address.

Control unit: the circuits in the CPU that sequence, interpret and carry out instructions.

Cybernetics: the science of control and communications systems founded on the theory that intelligent beings adapt to their environments and accomplish goals by reacting to feedback from their surroundings. Cybernetic theories became the basis of neural-modeling, or bottom-up, AI research.

Data base: an organized collection of facts about a subject.

Data bus: the pathway along which information and instructions must travel when moving between a computer's memory and its central processing unit.

Data structure: the form in which knowledge is stored in a computer.

Deductive reasoning: the process of working from given premises to a specific conclusion.

Digital: pertaining to the representation, manipulation or transmission of information by discrete, or on-off, signals.

Digital computer: a machine that operates on data expressed in discrete, or on-off, form rather than the continuous representation used in an analog computer.

Digitize: to represent data in digital, or discrete, form or to convert an analog, or continuous, signal to such a form.

Discovery learning: an unsupervised type of inductive learning that involves observing events and manipulating concepts, then forming new theories and concepts without help from an external source.

Distributed memory: memory that is distributed throughout the structure of a neural network rather than localized in a single place, as in a serial computer.

Domain: the specific subject or area of expertise covered by an AI program such as an expert system or a learning program.

Edge detection: the process of recording places on a digitized image where brightness values change abruptly; such locations usually correspond to an edge.

Expert system: a program that generates advice and makes limited decisions within a given domain by drawing on a knowledge base of detailed information about that domain.

Expert-system shell: a general-purpose expert system containing reasoning mechanisms and a skeletal knowledge base into which a user can inject specialized knowledge.

Feature extraction: an approach to object recognition in which an object is classified by its identifying features.

Fifth-generation computer: an experimental, non-von Neumann, parallel-processing computer.

Frame: a data structure, stored in a computer program, that describes an object or concept by enumerating its attributes and associated values; *see* Slot.

Front-end program: a program that allows nonexperts to retrieve information from a specialized data base by asking questions in a natural language.

Gray-level array: two-dimensional measurements of the amount of light reflected into a camera from points on the surfaces of three-dimensional objects.

Heuristics: rules of thumb or good judgment, based on experience, that humans and computers use to narrow the search for the solution of a problem.

Hill climbing: a problem-solving search stragegy in which an estimate of the distance to the goal is used to order the choices so that the most promising possibilities are explored first.

If-then rules: simple statements of logic employed by AI programs such as expert systems and learning programs.

Inductive learning: the process of learning by observing examples, extracting essential features and generalizing from these specifics to form new concepts.

Inference engine: the section of an expert-system program that contains its logic.

Knowledge base: a data base used in AI applications that consists of facts, inferences and procedures needed to solve a problem.

Knowledge-based system: *see* Expert system.

Knowledge engineer: a computer specialist who translates a human expert's knowledge about a particular subject into a format that can be processed by an expert system.

Knowledge representation: a means of organizing human knowledge into a data structure that can include rules, facts and common sense.

Learning machine: a machine that can monitor its own behavior and employ feedback to modify that behavior; also called an adaptive network or a self-organizing system.

Links: the connecting devices that join the nodes in a semantic net; each link has a meaning in its own right indicating the relationships among nodes.

LISP: (for List Processing) a widely used AI-programming language that manipulates nonnumerical symbols, particularly English words and phrases, which it can then link into complex hierarchies of thought.

Machine learning: the process by which a computer increases its knowledge and changes its own behavior as the result of its experience and past performance.

Machine vision: the process by which a computer perceives or recognizes objects in the external world.

Memory: the storage facilities of a computer; the term is applied only to internal storage as opposed to external storage, such as disks or tapes.

Morphemics: rules describing how words are changed to form variations such as plurals or verb conjugations.

Natural language: ordinary human language; unlike precisely defined computer languages, it is often ambiguous and is thus interpreted differently by different hearers.

Natural-language processing: software that effects a two-way translation between ordinary human language and a structure that computers understand.

Neural modeling: *see* Bottom-up theory.

Neural network: a collection of neurons linked together in such a way that individual neurons can perform separate functions simultaneously.

Neuron: the fundamental active cell in all animal nervous systems.

Node: an individual object, concept or event in a semantic net.

Parallel processor: a computer that is capable of performing multiple operations at the same time.

Pattern matching: comparing input with images or templates in a data base.

Perceptron: a prototype pattern-recognition machine modeled on the human nervous system.

Phonemes: the basic sounds of human speech.

Phonemics: rules describing variations in pronunciation that occur when spoken words are run together.

Phonetics: the physical characteristics of the sound patterns in words.

Pixel: short for ''picture element''; one of the thousands of points on a computer screen from which digital images are formed.

Program: a sequence of detailed instructions for performing some operation or solving some problem by computer.

Prosodics: rules for interpreting variations in stress and intonation in speech.

Rote learning: a type of learning in which all knowledge is explicitly provided by an external source, as by programmers in conventional computer programming.

Rule-based system: *see* Expert system.

Script: a framelike structure used to represent a sequence of events.

Search: a procedure for automated problem solving in which a computer seeks a solution by selecting among various possible alternatives.

Search tree: a hierarchical arrangement of choices used in solving a problem through search.

Semantic net: a knowledge-representation scheme that organizes human knowledge into a weblike structure consisting of nodes — objects, concepts and events — connected by links that specify the nature of the connections.

Semantics: the study of the meaning of words.

Serial processor: a conventional computer composed of a memory connected by a data bus to a central processing unit that performs operations sequentially.

Slot: an element of a frame that is filled with descriptive information about a particular object or concept.

Smoothing: a preliminary step in edge detection in which minor fluctuations in the brightness values of a digitized image are averaged out in order to create a cleaner edge map.

Stereo vision: a means of perceiving three-dimensional shapes based on the disparity between two images taken from different perspectives.

Syntax: the rules, or grammar, of sentence formation.

Template matching: a technique in which a computer identifies objects by comparing shapes derived from the digitized image with stored prototype patterns.

Top-down theory: an approach to AI based on the belief that human intelligence is best simulated by complex programming that mimics human thought processes.

Turing test: a criterion for machine intelligence maintaining that a computer is intelligent if it can deceive a human tester into believing that it is human.

Very-large-scale integrated circuit: a type of computer chip containing hundreds of thousands of transistors and other components on a single sliver of silicon.

Von Neumann architecture: standard computer design based on stored programs and sequential processing; *see* Serial processor.

Von Neumann bottleneck: the funneling of the flow of information into a single channel between the CPU and memory in a serial processor.

Picture Credits

Bibliography

Books

Aleksander, Igor, and Piers Burnett, *Reinventing Man: The Robot Becomes Reality*. New York: Holt, Rinehart and Winston, 1983.

Barr, Avron, Paul Cohen and Edward A. Feigenbaum, eds., *The Handbook of Artificial Intelligence*. 3 vols. Los Altos, Calif.: William Kaufmann, 1982.

Belzer, Jack, Albert G. Holzman and Allen Kent, eds., *Encyclopedia of Computer Science and Technology*. Vol. 7. New York: Marcell Dekker, 1978.

Bernstein, Jeremy, *Science Observed: Essays out of My Mind*. New York: Basic Books, 1982.

Boden, Margaret A., *Artificial Intelligence and Natural Man*. New York: Basic Books, 1977.

Bolter, J. David, *Turing's Man: Western Culture in the Computer Age*. Chapel Hill, N.C.: University of North Carolina Press, 1984.

Buchanan, Bruce G., and Edward H. Shortliffe, eds., *Rule-Based Expert Systems: The MYCIN Experiments of the Stanford Heuristic Programming Project*. Reading, Mass.: Addison-Wesley, 1983.

Chapuis, Alfred, and Edmond Droz, *Automata: A Historical and Technological Study*. Transl. by Alec Reid. London: B. T. Batsford, 1958.

Dreyfus, Hubert L., *What Computers Can't Do: A Critique of Artificial Reason*. New York: Harper & Row, 1972.

Feigenbaum, Edward A., and Pamela McCorduck, *The Fifth Generation: Artificial Intelligence and Japan's Computer Challenge to the World*. Reading, Mass.: Addison-Wesley, 1983.

Gevarter, William B., *Intelligent Machines: An Introductory Perspective of Artificial Intelligence and Robotics*. Englewood Cliffs, N.J.: Prentice-Hall, 1985.

Harmon, Paul, and David King, *Expert Systems: Artificial Intelligence in Business*. New York: John Wiley & Sons, 1985.

Hayes-Roth, Frederick, Donald A. Waterman and Douglas B. Lenat, eds., *Building Expert Systems*. Reading, Mass.: Addison-Wesley, 1983.

Helmers, Carl T., ed., *Robotics Age: In the Beginning*. Hasbrouck Heights, N.J.: Hayden Book Company, 1983.

Hillis, W. Daniel, *The Connection Machines*. Cambridge, Mass.: M.I.T. Press, 1985.

Hilts, Philip J., *Scientific Temperaments: Three Lives in Contemporary Science*. New York: Simon and Schuster, 1984.

Hinton, Geoffrey E., and James A. Anderson, *Parallel Models of Associative Memory*. Hillsdale, N.J.: Lawrence Erlbaum Associates, 1981.

Hodges, Andrew, *Alan Turing: The Enigma*. New York: Simon & Schuster, 1983.

Hofstadter, Douglas R., *Godel, Escher, Bach: An Eternal Golden Braid*. New York: Vintage Books, 1980.

Jacker, Corinne, *Man, Memory, and Machines: An Introduction to Cybernetics*. New York: Macmillan, 1964.

Johnson-Laird, P. N., and P. C. Wason, *Thinking*. Cambridge: Cambridge University Press, 1977.

Lea, Wayne A., ed., *Trends in Speech Recognition*. Englewood Cliffs, N.J.: Prentice-Hall, 1980.

McCorduck, Pamela, *Machines Who Think*. New York: W. H. Freeman, 1979.

Michalski, Ryszard S., Jaime G. Carbonell and Tom M. Mitchell, eds., *Machine Learning: An Artificial Intelligence Approach*. Palo Alto, Calif.: Tioga Publishing, 1983.

Michie, Donald, ed., *Introductory Readings in Expert Systems*. New York: Gordon and Breach Science Publishers, 1982.

Minsky, Marvin, ed., *Semantic Information Processing*. Cambridge, Mass.: M.I.T. Press, 1968.

Norman, Donald A.:
Learning and Memory. San Francisco: W. H. Freeman, 1982.
Memory and Attention: An Introduction to Human Information Processing. New York: John Wiley & Sons, 1969.

Pylyshyn, Zenon, ed., *Perspectives on the Computer Revolution*. Englewood Cliffs, N.J.: Prentice-Hall, 1970.

Rich, Elaine, *Artificial Intelligence*. New York: McGraw-Hill, 1983.

Ritchie, David, *The Binary Brain: Artificial Intelligence in the Age of Electronics*. Boston: Little, Brown, 1984.

Rose, Frank, *Into the Heart of the Mind*. New York: Harper & Row, 1984.

Rothfeder, Jeffrey, *Minds over Matter*. New York: Simon & Schuster, 1985.

Schank, Roger, *The Cognitive Computer*. Reading, Mass.: Addison-Wesley, 1984.

Weizenbaum, Joseph, *Computer Power and Human Reason: From Judgment to Calculation*. New York: W. H. Freeman, 1976.

Wiener, Norbert:
Cybernetics. Cambridge, Mass.: M.I.T. Press, 1961.
Ex-Prodigy: My Childhood and Youth. New York: Simon & Schuster, 1953.
The Human Use of Human Beings: Cybernetics and Society. Garden City, N.Y.: Doubleday, 1954.
I Am a Mathematician. Toronto: Doubleday, 1956.

Winston, Patrick Henry, *Artificial Intelligence*. Reading, Mass.: Addison-Wesley, 1984.

Winston, Patrick Henry, and Richard Henry Brown, eds., *Artificial Intelligence: An M.I.T. Perspective*. 2 vols. Cambridge, Mass.: M.I.T. Press, 1982.

Periodicals

Alexander, Tom:
"Artificial Intelligence." *Popular Computing*, May 1985.
"Computers on the Road to Self-Improvement." *Fortune*, June 14, 1982.
"Practical Uses for 'Useless' Science." *Fortune*, May 31, 1982.
"Teaching Computers the Art of Reason." *Fortune*, May 17, 1982.

Alpert, William, "Computers with Smarts: AI, an Infant Technology with Vast Promise." *Barron's*, January 23, 1984.

"Artificial Intelligence Is Here." *Business Week*, July 9, 1984.

Ballard, Dana H., and Christopher M. Brown, "Vision." *BYTE*, April 1985.

Barnard, Stephen T., and Martin A. Fischler, "Computational Stereo." *Computing Surveys*, December 1982.

Bernstein, Jeremy, "Profiles: A.I." *The New Yorker*, December 14, 1981.

Bobrow, Daniel G., ed., "Generalization as Search." *Artificial Intelligence: An International Journal* (Amsterdam), March 1982.

"Boeing Accelerates Research Dissemination of Technology." *Aviation Week & Space Technology*, February 17, 1986.

Bolter, J. David, "Artificial Intelligence." *Daedalus*, Summer 1984.

Brachman, Ronald J., "What Is-A Is and Isn't: An Analysis of Taxonomic Links in Semantic Networks." *Computer*, October 1983.

"The Brainchild of Today's Computer." *The Economist,* December 11, 1982.

Butz, J. S., Jr., "Electronic Device Simulates Processes of Human Brain." *Aviation Week,* July 7, 1958.

"DARPA's Pilot's Associate Program Provides Development Challenges." *Aviation Week & Space Technology,* February 17, 1986.

Davis, Bob, "Road to Reasoning." *The Wall Street Journal,* February 11, 1986.

Davis, Dwight B., "English: The Newest Computer Language." *High Technology,* February 1984.

Douglas, John H., "New Computer Architectures Tackle Bottleneck." *High Technology,* June 1983.

Duda, Richard O., and John G. Gaschnig, "Knowledge-Based Expert Systems Come of Age." *BYTE,* September 1981.

Duda, Richard O., and Edward H. Shortliffe, "Expert Systems Research." *Science,* April 15, 1983.

Edelson, Edward, "Expert Systems: Computers That Think like People." *Popular Science,* November 1982.

Fersko-Weiss, Henry, "Expert Systems: Decision-Making Power." *Personal Computing,* November 1985.

Fikes, Richard, and Tom Kehler, "The Role of Frame-Based Representation in Reasoning." *Communications of the ACM,* September 1985.

Gevarter, William B., "Expert Systems: Limited but Powerful." *IEEE Spectrum,* August 1983.

Ham, Michael, "Playing by the Rules." *PC World,* January 1984.

Hansen, James, "The Clockmaker's Androids." *Science 82,* July/August 1982.

Hartmann, Thom, "Adding Vision to Computers." *Popular Computing,* September 1984.

Herman, Ros, "Computers on the Road to Intelligence." *New Scientist,* August 5, 1982.

"Heuristics." *The New Yorker,* August 29, 1959.

Hilts, Philip J.:
"The Dean of Artificial Intelligence." *Psychology Today,* January 1983.
"John McCarthy." *OMNI,* April 1983.

"Human Brains Replaced?" *Newsweek,* July 21, 1958.

Kaarsberg, Tina, "Artificial Intelligence: Software Sophistry." *Yale Scientific,* Spring 1981.

Kinnucan, Paul:
"Artificial Intelligence: Making Computers Smarter." *High Technology,* November/December 1982.
"Computers That Think like Experts." *High Technology,* January 1984.
"Machines That See." *High Technology,* April 1983.

Klass, Philip J., "Perceptron Shows Its Ability to Learn." *Aviation Week & Space Technology,* July 4, 1960.

Kolcum, Edward H., "NASA Demonstrates Use of AI with Expert Monitoring System." *Aviation Week & Space Technology,* March 17, 1986.

Kotulak, Ronald, "New Machine Will Type Out What It 'Hears.'" *Chicago Tribune,* June 18, 1963.

Langley, Pat, and Jaime G. Carbonell, "Approaches to Machine Learning." *Journal of the American Society for Information Science,* 1984.

La Plante, Alice, "Talking with Your Computer." *Infoworld,* January 13, 1985.

Le Brecque, Mort, "The Tantalizing Quest for Speech Recognition Computers." *Popular Science,* July 1983.

Lenat, Douglas B., "Computer Software for Intelligent Systems." *Scientific American,* September 1984.

McCalla, Gordon, and Nick Nercone, "Approaches to Knowledge Representation." *Computer,* October 1983.

"Machine Learns Alphabet." *Science News Letter,* July 2, 1960.

"Machine Vision: Knowing What to Look for." *The Economist,* June 25, 1983.

McKean, Kevin, "Consulting the Electronic Experts." *Discover,* October 1984.

Marr, David, and H. Keith Nishihara, "Visual Information Processing: Artificial Intelligence and the Sensorium of Sight." *Technology Review,* October 1978.

"Memories Are Made of This." *The Economist,* August 10, 1985.

Minsky, Marvin, "Why People Think Computers Can't." *Technology Review,* November/December 1983.

Nelson, Ruth, "The First Literate Computers?" *Psychology Today,* March 1978.

"New Navy Device Learns by Doing." *The New York Times,* July 8, 1958.

Poggio, Tomaso, "Vision by Man and Machine." *Scientific American,* April 1984.

Rauch-Hindlin, Wendy, "Natural Language: An Easy Way to Talk to Computers." *Systems & Software,* January 1984.

Renkin, Andrew C., "Artificial Intelligence: Will Machines Ever Be Conscious?" *Science Digest,* October 1985.

"Researchers Channel AI Activities toward Real-World Applications." *Aviation Week & Space Technology,* February 17, 1986.

"Rival." *The New Yorker,* December 6, 1958.

Roberts, Steven K., "Artificial Intelligence." *BYTE,* September 1981.

Rothberg, Edward, "A Concerto for Artificial Intelligence." *The New York Times,* June 28, 1981.

Samuel, Arthur L.:
"Some Studies in Machine Learning Using the Game of Checkers." *IBM Journal of Research and Development,* July 1959.
"Some Studies in Machine Learning Using the Game of Checkers." Part 2, "Recent Progress." *IBM Journal of Research and Development,* November 1967.

Schank, Roger, and Larry Hunter, "The Quest to Understand Thinking." *BYTE,* April 1985.

Schrage, Michael, "Artificial Intelligence: Teaching Computers Power of Creative Stupidity." *The Washington Post,* December 1, 1985.

Shurkin, Joel N., "Expert Systems: The Practical Face of Artificial Intelligence." *Technology Review,* November/December 1983.

Simon, Herbert A., and Allen Newell, "Heuristic Problem-Solving: The Next Advance in Operations Research." *Operations Research,* January/February 1958.

Swearengin, Robert, "Parallel Processing." *Popular Computing,* May 1985.

Waldrop, M. Mitchell:
"Artificial Intelligence in Parallel." *Science,* August 10, 1984.
"Computer Vision." *Science,* June 15, 1984.
"The Fifth Generation: Taking Stock." *Science,* November 30, 1984.
"Machinations of Thought." *Science 85,* March 1985.
"Natural Language Understanding." *Science,* April 27, 1984.

West, Susan, "Beyond the One-Track Mind." *Science 85,* November 1985.

Winograd, Terry, "Computer Software for Working with Language." *Scientific American,* September 1984.

Other Publications

Automation & Robotics Panel, California Space Institute, University of California, "Automation & Robotics for the National Space Program." Washington, D.C.: NASA, February 25, 1985.

Committee on Science, Engineering, and Public Policy, National Academy of Science, "Research Briefings 1984." Washington, D.C.: National Academy Press, 1984.

Dyer, Michael G., "Restaurant Revisited, or Lunch with Boris." New Haven, Conn.: Computer Science Department, Yale University, no date.

Freitas, Robert A., and William P. Gilbreath, eds., *Advanced Auto-mation for Space Missions.* Washington, D.C.: NASA Scientific and Technical Information Branch, 1982.

Hildreth, Ellen C., "Edge Detection." Memo No. 858. Cambridge, Mass.: Artificial Intelligence Lab, M.I.T., September 1985.

The Home Computer Advanced Course. London: Orbis Publications, 1985.

Lenat, Douglas B., "Eurisko: Discovery of Heuristics by Heuristic Search." Palo Alto, Calif.: Heuristic Programming Project, Stanford University, January 1982.

Minsky, Marvin, "A Framework for Representing Knowledge: Artificial Intelligence." Memo No. 36. Cambridge, Mass.: Artificial Intelligence Lab, M.I.T., June 1974.

Schank, Roger, and Michael Lebowitz, "Levels of Understanding in Computers and People." Amsterdam: North-Holland Publishing, no date.

Acknowledgments

The index for this book was prepared by Mel Ingber. The editors also wish to thank: **In Canada:** Toronto — Hector Levesque, University of Toronto; **In the United States:** California — Beverly Hills: David Badley and Les Crane, Software Country; Irvine: Patrick Langley, University of California at Irvine; Los Angeles: Richard E. Korf, University of California at Los Angeles; Ramakant Nevatia, University of Southern California; Menlo Park: John Lowrence and Alex Pentland, SRI International; Moffett Field: Henry Lum, National Aeronautics and Space Administration; Palo Alto: Robert Engelmore, Stanford University; Judy Harris, Teknowledge; John Laird, Xerox Palo Alto Research Center; Pasadena: Geoffrey Fox, California Institute of Technology; San Diego: Theodore H. Bullock and David Criswell, University of California at San Diego; Stanford: Edward A. Feigenbaum and Arthur L. Samuel, Stanford University; District of Columbia: Lakita Conley and Barry G. Silverman, George Washington University; Florida — Cape Canaveral: John Jamieson, Kennedy Space Center, National Aeronautics and Space Administration; Illinois — Urbana: Ryszard S. Michalski, University of Illinois at Urbana-Champaign; Maryland — Baltimore: Neal J. Cohen, Johns Hopkins University; Bethesda: Jeffery Barker and David Lange, National Institutes of Health; College Park: Larry Davis, University of Maryland; Massachusetts — Amherst: Allen R. Hanson, University of Massachusetts; Cambridge: John Canny, John Rubin, Jon Wade and Richard Zippel, Massachusetts Institute of Technology; Connection Machine is a registered trademark of Thinking Machines Corporation; Lowell: Lou Tychonievich, Wang; New Jersey — New Brunswick: Thomas M. Mitchell and Jack Mostow, Rutgers University; New York — Ithaca: Howard Kurtzman, Cornell University; Pennsylvania — Pittsburgh: Harry E. Pople Jr., University of Pittsburgh; Larry Eshelman, Sandra Marcus, Raj Reddy, Herbert A. Simon, Charles E. Thorpe and Richard Wallace, Carnegie-Mellon University; Rhode Island — Providence: Stuart Geman, Brown University; Texas — Houston: Reg Berka, Johnson Space Flight Center, National Aeronautics and Space Administration; Virginia — Arlington: Alan Meyrowitz, Office of the Chief of Naval Research; Washington — Richland: Marvin Erickson, Battelle Northwest Pacific Labs; Seattle: Frederick J. Dickey and Amy L. Toussaint, Boeing Aerospace Company.

Index

Numerals in italics indicate an illustration of the subject mentioned.

A

Abelson, Robert, 69
AM (Automated Mathematician), 80
Anderson, James, 108
AQ11, 76
Arbib, Michael, 12
Arches, 75-76
Artificial intelligence: beginnings, 8-9; definition, 7; founders, 56-57; machine learning, 73-84; naming, 56-57; neural-modeling approach, 11-14, 103, 108-110; perception, 100-109; potential consequences, 7; in space, 111; thinking, 109-110

B

Babbage, Charles, 8
Backus, John, 102
BACON, 77, 80
Bigelow, Julian, 10
Binary numbers, and neurons, 11-12
Boltzmann machine, 109
Boole, George, 12
Bottom-up school, 7, 12-14, 103, 108
Buchanan, Bruce, 40

C

CADUCEUS, 40-41
Carnegie Institute of Technology (Carnegie-Mellon University), 9, 77
Certainty factors, 50-51
Chaining, backward, 48-49
Chaining, forward, 48
Checkers, 73-75
Chess, 8, 9
Chomsky, Noam, 59
Cimino, Aldo, 41-42
Colby, Kenneth, 59
Color analysis, *24-25*
Columbia University, 68
Combinatorial explosion, 34, *37*
Computer architecture: parallel, 103, *106-107*, 108-110; and perception, 102-103, 108-109; serial, 102-103, *104-105*
Conceptual dependency, 69
Connection Machine, 109
Connectivity map, *26-27*
Content addressability, 108
Cybernetics, 11-14, 103, 108
Cyc, 84
CYRUS, 70-71

D

DARPA (Defense Advanced Research Projects Agency), 100

Dartmouth College, Summer Research Project on Artificial Intelligence, 31, 42
DENDRAL, 39
DOCTOR, 58-59
Domain knowledge, 85, 86-87
Dreyfus, Hubert, 10

E

Edge detection, *18-19, 105, 106-107*
ELIZA, 58-59, 71
Empirical induction, 38
EMYCIN, 40
Eurisko, 81-83
Exhaustive search, 34, *37*
Expert systems, 9, 38-42, 43; certainty factors, 50-51; chaining, 48-49; chemical, 39; detective example, *44-53*; industrial, 41-42; limitations, 42, 75; medical, 40-41; in space, 111, 113

F

Fahlman, Scott, 64, 102-103, 109
Feature extraction, 26-27
Feedback, automatic, 10-11
Feigenbaum, Edward, 38-39, 40
Frames, 65, *66-67*, 81
Front-end programs, 61
Fuzzy concepts, 103

G

GPS (General Problem Solver), 35, 38

H

Hearsay II, 100-102
Heuristics, 34-35, 43, 74, 76, 85; search, 37
Hillis, Daniel, 109
Hinton, Geoffrey, 108, 109
Hooks and scars, 113

I

IBM: 701, 73-74; 704, 13
Image formation, *16-17*
IMIS (Intelligent Management Information System), 113
Inference engines, 40, 43

J

Jacquet-Droz, Pierre, 8

K

Knaus, Friedrich von, 8
Knowledge base, 43
Knowledge engineer, 41, 43
Knowledge representation, *62-63*, 64-65, *66-67*, 68-71; frames, 65, *66-67*, 81; MOPs, 70-71; scripts, 69; semantic network, *62-63*, 64-65

L

Langley, Patrick, 77
Language, programming, for AI, 56-57
Language comprehension, computer, 56-61, 64-65, 68-71; if-then rules, 71; knowledge representation, 64-65, 68-71; and semantics, 60-61, 64-65, 68-71; syntax approach, 56, 60-61
Language translation, computer, 55-56
Learning, *78-79*
Learning by discovery, 76-77, 80-84, 97
Learning by example, 75-76, 85, *86-97*; domain knowledge, 85, 86-87; learning task, 85, 86-87; overgeneralization, 94; overspecialization, 94; performance task, 85, 86-87
Lederberg, Joshua, 38-39
Lenat, Douglas, 77, 80-84
LES (Liquid Oxygen Expert System), 111
Links, *62-63*
LISP, 57-58, 81
Logic Theorist, 31-33, 34, 35

M

McCarthy, John, 56-57, 65, 67
McCulloch, Warren, 11, 12
Machine learning, 73-84, 97; by discovery, 76-77, 80-84, 97; by example, 75-76, 85, *86-97*
Mathematics, learning-program, 80-81, 85, *86-97*
MCC (Microelectronics and Computer Technology Corporation), 84
Medical expert systems, 40-41
Memory: content addressability, 108; distributed, 108; and knowledge representation, *62-63, 66-67*
Meyers, Jack, 41
Michalski, Ryszard, 76
Minsky, Marvin, 14, 42, 57, 65, 67-68, 99, 110
M.I.T. (Massachusetts Institute of Technology), 9, 57, 65
Moon, research and development on, *114-115*
Moravec, Hans, 110
Morphemics, 101
MYCIN, 40

N

Natural language, 55, 56, 61
Nealey, Robert W., 75
Neurons, electronic modeling of, 12-13, 103, 108-110
New connectionists, 109
Newell, Allen, 31, 32-33, 35, 39, 57, 100
Nilsson, Nils, 71
Nodes, *62-63*

O
Oettinger, Anthony G., 55
Overgeneralization, 94
Overspecialization, 94

P
Papert, Seymour, 14
Paracelsus (Theophrastus Bombastus von Hohenheim), 8
Parallel Models of Associative Memory, 103, 108
Parallel processing, 103, *106-107,* 108-110
Parser, 60
Perception, machine, 99-100; and computer architecture, 102-103, *104-107,* 108-110; memory, 108; speech recognition, 100-102; vision, 15, *16-29,* 102, 104, *105, 106-107*
Perceptrons, 12-14, 15, 109
Phonemics, 101
Phonetics, 101
Pitts, Walter, 11, 12
Pixels, *17*
Polya, George, 34
Pople, Harry, 41
Pragmatics, 101
Prosodics, 101

Q
Quillian, M. Ross, 64-65

R
RAND Corporation, 31
Random search, 37
Reddy, Raj, 100, 102
RLL (Representation Learning Language), 81

Robots in space, *114-119*
Rogers, Carl, 58
Rosenblatt, Frank, 12-13, 15, 109
Rule-based program, 39

S
SAM (Script-Applier Mechanism), 69-70
Samuel, Arthur, *73-75*
Schank, Roger, 68-71, 75, 109
Scripts, 69-70
Search methods, *36-37*
Searle, John R., 71
Sejnowsky, Terrence J., 109
Semantics, 60-61, 64-65, 68-71, 101; nets, *62-63*
Shannon, Claude, 12
Shaw, J. C., 31, *32-33,* 35, 100
Shortliffe, Edward, 40
SHRDLU, 60-61
Simon, Herbert A., 31-33, 34, 35, 39, 57, 77, 100
Smith, Michael, 41
Space exploration, 111; scenario, *112-119*
Speech recognition, 100-102. *See also* SUR
SRI International, 71
Stanford University, 9, 57
SUR (Speech Understanding Research), 100
Symbolic logic, program to prove theorems, 31-33
Syntax, 101; approach to language, 56, 59-61

T
Template matching, *26-27*
Texture analysis, *22-23*
Thinking, 108-109

Thinking Machines Corporation, 109
Three-dimensional vision, *20-21*
Time sharing, 57, 58
Top-down school, 7, 14
Torres y Quevedo, Leonardo, 8
Traveller TCS, 82-83
Tree, search, *36-37*
Turing, Alan, 7

U
University of California at Berkeley, 68
University of Illinois, 73

V
Vaucanson, Jacques de, 8
Vision, machine, 102, 104; color analysis, *24-25;* connectivity map, *26, 27;* difficulties, *28-29;* edge detection, *18-19, 105, 106-107;* feature extraction, *26-27;* image formation, *16-17;* object recognition, 15, *16-29;* relational approach, *26-27;* template matching, *26-27;* texture analysis, *22-23;* in three dimensions, *20-21*
Von Neumann, John, 102; architecture, *104-105*

W
Weaver, Warren, 55
Weizenbaum, Joseph, 58-59, 71
Wiener, Norbert, 10-11, 12
Winograd, Terry, 60
Winston, Patrick H., 75-76, 84

Y
Yale University, 68

Time-Life Books Inc.
is a wholly owned subsidiary of
TIME INCORPORATED

FOUNDER: Henry R. Luce 1898-1967

Editor-in-Chief: Henry Anatole Grunwald
President: J. Richard Munro
Chairman of the Board: Ralph P. Davidson
Corporate Editor: Ray Cave
Group Vice President, Books: Reginald K. Brack Jr.
Vice President, Books: George Artandi

TIME-LIFE BOOKS INC.

EDITOR: George Constable
Director of Design: Louis Klein
Editorial General Manager: Neal Goff
Director of Editorial Resources: Phyllis K. Wise
Acting Text Director: Ellen Phillips
Editorial Board: Dale M. Brown, Roberta Conlan,
Thomas H. Flaherty Jr., Donia Ann Steele, Rosalind
Stubenberg, Kit van Tulleken, Henry Woodhead
Director of Photography and Research:
John Conrad Weiser

PRESIDENT: Reginald K. Brack Jr.
Executive Vice Presidents: John M. Fahey Jr.,
Christopher T. Linen
Senior Vice President: James L. Mercer
Vice Presidents: Stephen L. Bair, Edward Brash,
Ralph J. Cuomo, Juanita T. James, Hallett Johnson III,
Robert H. Smith, Paul R. Stewart, Leopoldo Toralballa
Director of Production Services: Robert J. Passantino

Editorial Operations
Copy Chief: Diane Ullius
Editorial Operations: Caroline A. Boubin (manager)
Production: Celia Beattie
Quality Control: James J. Cox (director)
Library: Louise D. Forstall

Correspondents: Elisabeth Kraemer-Singh (Bonn);
Dorothy Bacon (London); Maria Vincenza Aloisi,
Josephine du Brusle (Paris); Ann Natanson (Rome).
Valuable assistance was also provided by: Milly
Trowbridge (London); Elizabeth Brown, Christina
Lieberman (New York).

UNDERSTANDING COMPUTERS

SERIES DIRECTOR: Roberta Conlan
Series Administrator: Loretta Britten

Editorial Staff for *Artificial Intelligence*
Designer: Robert K. Herndon
Associate Editors: Russell B. Adams Jr. (text),
Sara Schneidman (pictures)
Researchers: *Writer:*
Elisabeth Carpenter   Lydia Preston
Karen Monks
Pamela L. Whitney
Assistant Designers: Antonio Alcalá,
Christopher M. Register
Copy Coordinator: Anthony K. Pordes
Picture Coordinator: Renée DeSandies
Editorial Assistant: Miriam Newton Morrison

Special Contributors: Tom Alexander, Ronald H. Bailey,
Donal Kevin Gordon, Charles Smith, Daniel Stashower,
David Thiemann (text); Sara Mark (research)

CONSULTANTS

MARVIN MINSKY is the Donner Professor of Science at
the Massachusetts Institute of Technology and one of the
most influential leaders in the field of artificial intelligence. He researches general theories of intelligence and
knowledge representation at M.I.T.'s Artificial Intelligence Laboratory.

RONALD J. BRACHMAN heads the Artificial Intelligence
Principles Research Department at AT&T Bell Laboratories in New Jersey. One of his areas of research is knowledge representation.

JAIME G. CARBONELL is an associate professor of Computer Science at Carnegie-Mellon University whose research interests include natural-language interfaces, machine learning and analogical reasoning.

RANDALL DAVIS, an associate professor at the Massachusetts Institute of Technology, is on the faculty of the
Sloan School of Management and does research in expert
systems at M.I.T.'s Artificial Intelligence Laboratory.

MIKE DRUMHELLER is a member of the research staff at
Thinking Machines Corporation in Cambridge, Massachusetts. His areas of research are computer vision and
parallel processing.

CARL EBELING has a Ph.D. in Computer Science from
Carnegie-Mellon University. His interests are VLSI (very-
large-scale-integration) architecture, heuristic search and
computer chess.

RICHARD M. KELLER is a doctoral student specializing in
artificial intelligence and machine learning in the Computer Science Department of Rutgers University.

DOUGLAS B. LENAT is Principal Scientist of the Artificial
Intelligence Project at Microelectronics and Computer
Technology Corporation, Austin, Texas. His primary
areas of research are knowledge acquisition and learning.

CURTIS MARX is a graduate student researching natural
language in the Artificial Intelligence Laboratory at the
Massachusetts Institute of Technology.

ISABEL LIDA NIRENBERG has dealt with a wide range of
computer applications, from analysis of data collected by
the Pioneer space probes to the matching of children and
families for adoption agencies. She works at the Computer Center at the State University of New York at Albany.

STEVE SHAFER is a research scientist studying computer
vision in the Computer Science Department of Carnegie-
Mellon University.

HARRY L. VOORHEES is a computer scientist working in
the areas of computer vision, graphics and artificial intelligence at the Massachusetts Institute of Technology.

Library of Congress Cataloguing in Publication Data

Artificial intelligence
   (Understanding computers)
   Bibliography: p.
   Includes index
   1. Artificial intelligence. 2. Machine learning.
I. Time-Life Books.
II. Series.
Q335.A7855 1986   006.3   86-5765
ISBN 0-8094-5675-3
ISBN 0-8094-5671-1 (lib. bdg.)

For information about any Time-Life book, please write:
Reader Information
541 North Fairbanks Court
Chicago, Illinois 60611

Time-Life Books Inc. offers a wide range of fine recordings,
including a *Big Bands* series. For subscription information, call
1-800-621-7026, or write TIME-LIFE MUSIC, Time & Life
Building, Chicago, Illinois 60611.